D0899902

A Garland Series

RENAISSANCE DRAMA

A COLLECTION OF
CRITICAL EDITIONS

edited by
STEPHEN ORGEL
The Johns Hopkins University

A Pleasant Commodie Called Looke About You
A Critical Edition

RICHARD S. M. HIRSCH

Garland Publishing, Inc.
New York & London • 1980

All volumes in this series are printed on
acid-free, 250-year-life paper.

Library of Congress Cataloging in Publication Data

Look about you.
  A pleasant commodie called Looke about you.

  (Renaissance drama; 2d ser.)
  1. Look about you.   I. Hirsch, Richard S. M., 1945–
II. Series.
PR2411.L7   1980   822'.3   79-54343
ISBN 0-8240-4460-6

PRINTED IN THE UNITED STATES OF AMERICA

For

My   Parents

CONTENTS

Preface

THIS EDITION is the first in this series not to have been completed originally as a dissertation. In preparing my own dissertation for publication by the Renaissance English Text Society some years ago, I found that approximately ninety pages of the Introduction dropped away quite painlessly. I have therefore tried from the beginning in this edition of LOOKE ABOUT YOU to present only what seems necessary to the scholarly reader, and with as little fuss as possible, especially in the Introduction and Explanatory Notes. In the Textual Notes I have tried to include all details which a reader would need to reconstruct the substantive readings of the copy-text and the variant readings of its seven fellow-exemplars, including a representative sampling of their accidentals. The only other place where I have preferred copiousness to brevity is in the acknowledgments which follow.

The copy-text is reprinted by permisssion of the Folger Shakespeare Library, Washington, D. C., to which, and to its Director, Dr. O. B. Hardison, Jr., I am very grateful.

Throughout the twelve years which have elapsed since I first began work on this edition, I have been helped and encouraged by countless colleagues and friends, probably by more than I can now remember. Among the earliest was Professor George K. Anderson of Brown University, who first encouraged me in my belief that LOOKE ABOUT YOU is a lively and charming play, and one well worth editing.

Professor Sears Jayne, also of Brown, supplied excellent advice in the early stages of the project, and encouragement ever since. Messrs. James Claydon and Donald F. R. Missen, Under Librarians of the Univerity Library, Cambridge, helped me to find much that pertained to this play in the vast holdings of that insitution, and made me their friend in the process. The late Professor Sir Frank Adcock, of King's College, Cambridge, helped me to avoid some of the many pitfalls in the path of the young editor, and also gave me the benefit of his own very personal view of the play. Professor William Beattie, Librarian of the National Library of Scotland, was extremely helpful in having a reproduction of the NLS copy made for me while I was in Edinburgh.

The Rockefeller Library, Brown University, very

generously helped by adding to its collections reproductions
of the copy-text and the other copies of the 1600 text for the
purpose of my collating them, and has since proved very
generous and prompt in sending these copies out to me on
inter-library loan. In this connection I must thank another
friend, Professor Stuart C. Sherman, John Hay Librarian at
Brown University, who has always helped me, as he has helped
so many others, with warmth, grace, and a real dedication to
learning.

I am particularly indebted to the Southeastern Institute
of Medieval and Renaissance Studies for electing me to a
Fellowship for the Summer of 1975 at the University of North
Carolina at Chapel Hill, and to Professor David M. Bevington
of the University of Chicago, both for selecting me for the
Seminar on Shakespeare and Early Drama of which he was Senior
Fellow that summer, and, in common with with my fellow seminar
members, for spending much time and effort improving my
edition with many corrections and much good advice.

Professor A. S. C. Edwards of the University of Victoria
was kind enough to bring my edition to the notice of Garland
Publishing, Inc.

Professor Anne B. Lancashire of University College,
University of Toronto, has been most generous in giving me
permission to quote from the apparatus of her unpublished
modern spelling dissertation-edition done at Harvard in 1965.
I am also very grateful to her for telling me of a production
of LOOKE ABOUT YOU staged in Toronto in the summer of 1977,
and for putting me in touch with its director, Mr. Jonathan
Rittenhouse, of the Graduate Centre for the Study of Drama,
University of Toronto, who very kindly sent me further details
of what must have been a most charming production.

My greatest, albeit my most recent, debt is to my
colleague Professor Victor Culver, who by his great generosity
in making available to me his IMSAI 8080 computer, and his
great patience in teaching me how to use it, has made possible
the publication of this book in its present form. I am also
very grateful to his lovely wife Johanna, and to their
beautiful children Jenny and George, for very kindly making me
welcome over the many weeks when I worked in their home, and
for bearing with so much equanimity the many late nights and
much inconvenience which the typesetting and correction of
this work in their midst must have caused them.

To all of the above, and to everyone else who has helped
me in bringing this work to completion, my great thanks, and
my assurance that, if despite all their efforts, some errors
still remain herein, they are mine, not theirs.

R. S. M. H.

October 1979

Introduction

LOOKE ABOUT YOU is an interesting and quite delightful late Elizabethan comedy of unknown authorship. It seems to have achieved its artistic success by combining three kinds of dramatic entertainment which were particularly popular on the London stage in the late 1590's: History, comedy, and moral romance.

The setting of the play is historical: the dispute in 1173-74 between Henry II and his wife and sons (one of whom, Prince Henry, his father has unwisely had crowned in his own lifetime). King Henry, Elinor of Aquitaine, and their sons young King Henry, Richard and John all appear as characters (Geoffrey is mentioned, but for some reason is absent from the action).

Much is made of the historical situation (especially in the second, sixth, and last scenes, which take place at Court), but the actual comic action of the play concerns the attempts to escape from their respective enemies of two other characters, neither of whom is strictly historical.

The first of these is Robert, Earl of Gloucester, an actual historical figure, the bastard son of Henry I, and uncle of Henry II, but one who is used in this play quite outside his historical lifetime, since he died in 1147.(1) (One natural result of his anachronistic presence in the play is that, though he is clearly a member of the royal family, his exact relationship to the other members is left unclear.)

The second historical figure is Skinke (he is given no Christian name), the fictitious murderer of Rosamond, Henry II's mistress; he is clever, ruthless, good at disguises, and functions as an excellent foil for Gloucester.

The real action of the play is the comedy generated by the assumption of numerous disguises by Skinke and Gloucester as they try to escape from their enemies (the party of old King Henry for Skinke; the party of young King Henry for Gloucester). The multiple disguises, of course, soon become more general, as Lady Faulconbridge, the young and beautiful sister of Gloucester and wife of an elderly retainer of the old King, disguises herself so that she can visit the Hermit (actually Skinke in disguise) to learn her brother's whereabouts, and leaves young Robin Hood, Earl of Huntington, disguised as herself while she is away.

The names Robin Hood and Lady Faulconbridge will alert the reader familiar with Elizabethan drama that in LOOKE ABOUT YOU one finds the sort of historical backtracking that Shakespeare employed in THE MERRY WIVES OF WINDSOR. Robin Hood, the legendary English outlaw, who first appeared as Earl of Huntington in THE DOWNFALL and THE DEATH OF ROBERT EARL OF HUNTINGTON (1598), appears in LOOKE ABOUT YOU as a much younger figure, no more than a boy, and still in the wardship of Prince Richard. Similarly, Lady Faulconbridge, whom legend held to have borne King Richard a bastard son (Philip Faulconbridge, who, along with his mother, appears in Shakespeare's KING JOHN [c. 1594-95]), appears in LOOKE ABOUT YOU as a chaste young matron who, rather than yielding to Richard's suit, converts it from adulterous desire to courtly love. By this process of historical backtracking, LOOKE ABOUT YOU not only manages to capitalize on the Robin Hood material in the Huntington plays, but also preserves the character of Prince Richard by presenting him as an essentially positive force in the play (the only one of the royal sons to be so treated). By revising, or at least putting off, the outcome of his infatuation with Lady Faulconbridge, the anonymous author not only no doubt enhanced the play's popularity by affirming the goodness of a character who was, in popular legend, a notable symbol of English chivalry and kingliness, but also provided an ending that was at once romantic, happy, and moral.

Although the genre of LOOKE ABOUT YOU is at least as much multiple-disguise comedy as it is serious history, and seems to lie rather with JOHN A KENT AND JOHN A CUMBER (1590), THE BLIND BEGGAR OF ALEXANDRIA (1595-96), and THE BLIND BEGGAR OF BEDNAL GREEN (1600), than with 1 and 2 HENRY IV and HENRY V, the historical information in the play is drawn rather carefully from the chronicles, and, as Anne B. Lancashire has shown in an excellent article (2), the play is in several ways patterned after 1 HENRY IV. (See discussion of sources below.)

The historical scenes at Court, though only three in number, organize the entire play, and contain strong emphasis on the difference between good and bad rulers. Thus, Elinor of Aquitaine, the Frenchwoman, seems to stand for personal and autocratic rule (11. 2991-2996):

> Heare me Sonne Henry, while thou art a King,
> Give, take, pryson, thy subjects are thy slaves.
> Lift meek to thrones: proud hearts in dungions fling.
> Grace men today, to morrowe give them graves.
> A King must be like Fortune; ever turning,
> The world his football, all her glory spurning.

while in opposition to this King Henry II seems to care most for the well-being of his subjects, referring to his queen as (11. 226-231):

> Cruell Elinor ... my uncivill Queene;
> The Tygresse that hath drunke the purple bloud,
> Of three times twenty thousand valiant men;
> Washing her red chaps, in the weeping teares,
> Of widdows, virgins, nurses, sucking babes.

Henry the son, whom Elinor has bred up for the throne, accordingly cares nothing for the law or for the common good (ll. 1035-39):

FAUKENBRIDGE: Heere is a statute from the Confessor.

HENRY: The Confessor was but a simple foole.
Away with bookes my word shall be a lawe,
England her breath shall from this bosome drawe.
Gloster shall die...

In this the Elinor of Aquitaine of LOOKE ABOUT YOU is reminiscent of the Elinor of Castile in Peele's EDWARD I, another foreign queene, in this case Spanish, who wanted to impose continental autocracy on the English people.

Prince John, of the historical characters, is most satirized, and clearly is the least reliable of the three sons. This is perhaps not surprising, since the king on whose reputation the character is modeled was best known in the popular consciousness for having surrendered the crown of England to the Pope, a circumstance that would not endear him to the aggressively anti-Catholic Elizabethans.

Thus, in the tradition of the HENRY VI plays, LOOKE ABOUT YOU echoes primarily English patriotic concerns -- the rule of English, rather than foreign princes (e.g. the young King Henry sends his French royal bride home with her dowry after his surprising last-scene conversion); public-spirited rather than autocratic rule; and the maintenance of justice in small matters as well as great (the pardon and reinstatement of the porter of the Fleet Prison as well as of the Earl of Gloucester).

The historical scenes in LOOKE ABOUT YOU may in fact be considered a study of kingship in the negative terms in the sense that Shakespeare's second tetralogy is a study of it in positive terms. Moreover, Professor Lancashire's article (pp. 331-34) has shown that the play may well speak specifically to English political problems of the late 1590's. Her thesis is that the rebellious son Henry is intended to be seen as the Earl of Essex, Elizabeth I's favorite, and that the doting father represents the elderly Elizabeth herself. By discussing the many parallels between the factions surrounding Elizabeth and Essex and those surrounding the old King and the young King in LOOKE ABOUT YOU, and furthermore by showing what sort of historical details from the chronicles were left out of LOOKE ABOUT YOU, apparently in order to make the Henry-Essex parallel even more striking, Professor Lancashire rather convincingly demonstrates that the anonymous author seems to have intended that the audience should recognize an obvious similarity between the rebellion of young Henry in LOOKE ABOUT YOU and the feared rebellion of Essex, which, as Mrs. Lancashire points out, actually did come, and only about a year after the publication of the play.

Professor Lancashire concludes (p. 333) that "LOOK ABOUT YOU is thus very much a history play, and not merely a multiple-disguise comedy in which the author uses historical names and settings only for the sake of convenience or of additional box-office appeal."

Once this fact is granted, and I think that Mrs. Lancashire has shown that it must be, what is remarkable about the play is the skill with which the anonymous author has woven together the historical, comedic and romantic elements ino a unified and well-constructed whole, and put it on the stage in language which is remarkably versatile and strong.

In most historical comedies of the period, including 1 and 2 HENRY IV, only one or two "serious" historical characters are allowed to enter the subplot and the comic scenes; in this play only a few are kept out of them. King Henry, Queen Elinor and their reigning son Henry, as royal and ruling figures, naturally enough do not appear in the farcical disguise scenes, but every other member of the cast is somehow involved in the sixteen multiple disguises which fill the sixteen central scenes of the play. Prince John has his hat and cloak stolen by Skinke, who has been taken to the Fleet disguised as Redcap, but leaves disguised as John; Gloucester escapes as Redcap, but is soon disguised as Faulconbridge; Lady Faulconbridge disguises herself as a merchant's wife to visit the Hermit for news of her brother Gloucester, and Prince Richard comes a-courting his young ward Robin Hood, who has been left disguised as Lady Faulconbridge while she is away; both Skinke and Gloucester disguise themselves (sometimes simultaneously) as the Hermit; Prince Richard then disguises himself as a servingman to search for Gloucester, and ends by fighting with him in his disguise as the Hermit; John and Faulconbridge are both cozened by the Hermit played by Skinke, then robbed by Skinke disguised as a falconer, and then, supposing that they have discovered that the Hermit is Skinke, return to his cell only to be cozened by the Hermit played by Gloucester.

These are only some of the many disguises, but even these are enough to suggest how thoroughly the historical and comic plots are integrated with the romantic one.

The mainspring of the action is the "humourous" Earl of Gloucester, who throughout represents fun, honor, indecorum, patriotism, and the loyal criticism of his rightful monarch.

Though he does his best to escape Henry's "justice" and John's hatred, once captured he is contemptuous of their intended punishment (the loss of his hand and head): "Tut, I

am ready, to thy worst I dare thee." (1. 3104). His courage
sees to be the deciding factor in the young king's conversion,
and the return to the "working monarchy" that Gloucester has
called for all through the play.

   Given that the historical Earl Robert was dead long before
any of the historical events in the play took place, it seems
likely that, whatever other dramatic sources he may have had,
LOOKE ABOUT YOU's Earl Robert owes something at least to the
legend of another Lord of Gloucester, the "good Duke Humphrey"
of Shakespeare's 1 HENRY VI, who was literally, as Gloucester
in LOOKE ABOUT YOU is figuratively, the protector of the
monarchy.

SOURCES

   As Mrs. Lancashire has shown (pp. 321-31), the source of
most of the historical information in the play is Holinshed's
CHRONICLES OF ENGLAND, SCOTLAND, AND IRELAND. The most
relevant passages are reprinted below: (3)

   Therefore to preuent the chances of fortune, he [King
   Henry] determined whilest he was aliue to crowne his
   eldest sonne Henrie, being now of the age of 17 yeares,
   and so to inuest him in the kingdome by his owne act in
   his life time: which deed turned him to much trouble,
   as after shall appeare...
   Upon the daie of coronation, king Henrie the father
   serued his sonne at the table as sewer...Thus the Yoong
   man of an euill and peruerse nature, was puffed vp in
   pride by his fathers vnseemelie dooings....
   The king his father hearing his talke, was verie sor-
   rowfull in his mind..For he gessed hereby what a one he
   would prooue afterward, that shewed himselfe so dis-
   obedient and froward alreadie. But although he was dis-
   pleased with himselfe in that he had doone vndiscreet-
   lie, yet now when that which was doone could not be
   undoone, he caused all the Nobles and lords of the
   realme....to doo homage vnto his said sonne thus made
   fellow with him in the kingdome: but he would not
   release them of their oth of allegiance, wherein they
   stood bound to obeie him the father, so long as he
   liued.
                          1172
   [In 1172 the young king went to the French Court.]
   Neuerthelesse, whilest this yoong prince soiourned in
   France, king Lewes not hartilie fauouring the king of
   England, and therewithall perceiuing the rash and head-
   strong disposition of the yong king did first of all
   inuegle him to consider of his estate, and to remember
   that he was now a king equall vnto his father, and
   therefore aduised him so shortlie as he could, to get
   the entire gouernment out of his fathers hands: where-

vnto he furthermore promised all the aid that laie in
him to performe.

The yong king being readie inough not onelie to worke
vnquietnesse, but also to follow his father in lawes
counsell (as he that was apt of nature to aspire to the
sole gouernement, and loth to haue any partener in
authoritie..and namelie such one as might controll him)
was the more encouraged thereto by a number of prodigal
currie fauours....Herevpon the youthfull courage of the
yong king being tickled, began to wax of a contrarie
mind to his father....(HOLINSHED, II, 144)

                          1173
[Eventually the young king rose is rebellion against
his father.] Now whilest the father went about to as-
swage the sonnes displeasure, the mother queene Elianor
did what she could to pricke him forward in his dis-
obedient attempts. For she being enraged against hir
husband bicause he kept sundrie concubines, and therefore delited the lesse in hir companie, cared not what
mischeefe she procured against him. Herevpon she made
hir complaint so greeuouslie vnto hir sons Richard and
Geffrey, that they joined with their brother against
their father. (HOLINSHED, II, 149)

                          1174
[Military losses forced Richard to make peace with
his father.] His father most courteously receiuing him,
made so much of him as though he had not offended at
all. (HOLINSHED, II, 161)

[The Old King continued victorious over his sons'
forces, and the final result was] mutual attonement and
reconciliation wouen between the father and the sonnes;
their remorse for their vndutifulnes, his louing fauour
and gratiousnesse; their promptnesse to yeeld to condi-
tions of agreement, his forwardnes to giue consent to
couenants required; their readinesse to do the old king
homage, his acceptable admission of their proferred
seruice. (HOLINSHED, II, 168)

These passages are echoed in LOOKE ABOUT YOU by references
to the young king's coronation (11. 2553-57); the oath still
binding the nobility to the old King (1. 107); the fighting in
France (11. 148-150); and the French nationality of the young
queen (11. 3100, 3150).

Also mentioned in both Holinshed and LOOKE ABOUT YOU are
the small provision made by the King for his sons' support
(Holinshed, II, 148; LAY 11. 210-211); the tendency of the
young king to appropriate the lands of others for his own and
his servants' use (Holinshed, II, 148; LAY 11. 332-3); and
Prince Richard's vow to lead a crusade to the Holy Land
(Holinshed, II, 271: LAY 11. 247-252; 3167-3174).

The closest resemblance between LOOKE ABOUT YOU's use of the historical materials and Holinshed's account of them comes at the point of the young king's repentance, which the anonymous author of the play seems to have imitated closely from Holinshed's account of the young king's death:

Moreouer when he perceiued present death at hand, he first confessed his sinnes secretlie, and after openly before sundry bishops and men of religion, and receiued absolution in most humble wise. After this, he caused his fine clothes to be taken from him, and therewith a heare cloth to be put vpon him, and after tieng [sic] a cord about his necke, he said vnto the bishops and other that stood by him; "I deliuer my selfe an vn worthie and greeuous sinner vnto you the ministers of God by this cord, beseeching our Lord Jesus Christ, which pardoned the theefe confessing his faults on the crosse, that through your praiers and for his great mercies sake it may please him to be mercifull vnto my soule;" wherevnto they all answered, "Amen." Then he said vnto them, "Draw me out of this bed with this cord, and laie me on that bed strawed with ashes..." And so after he had receiued the sacrament of the bodie and bloud of our Lord, he departed this life as afore is said, about the 28. yeare of his age. (HOLINSHED, II, 185; A.D. 1183)

HENRY: Father, you see your most rebellious sonne,
Stricken with horror of his horred guilt,
Requesting sentence fitting his desart,
O treade upon his head, that trode your heart.
I doe deliver up all dignity,
Crowne, Scepter, swoord, unto your Majesty....
Send hence that Frenchwoman, give hr her dowry,
Let her not speake to trouble my milde soule,
Which of this world hath taken its last leave:
And by her power, will my proude flesh controule.
Off with these silkes, my garments shall be gray,
My shirt hard hayre, my bed the ashey dust,
My pillow but a lumpe of hardned clay:
For clay I am, and unto clay I must.
O I beseech ye let me goe alone,
To live, where my loose life I may bemone....
Farewell, farewell, the world is yours, pray take it.
ILe leave vexation, and with joy forsake it.
          (LOOKE ABOUT YOU 11. 3130-3135; 3150-3159; 3163-4)

While the historical information seems to have come mainly from Holinshed, the dramatic treatment of this information seems, as Mrs. Lancashire shows in her dissertation (pp. 45-46), to have come chiefly from Shakespeare's 1 HENRY IV. The similarities between the two works are striking: both 1 HENRY

IV AND LAY have tavern scenes, which contain both high and low characters, and a young drawer who constantly cries "Anon" and refers to swearing on the Bible. Then Faukenbridge, in scene xv of LOOKE ABOUT YOU, when his lady reveals her true identity to him, responds exactly as Falstaff does in 1 HENRY IV when he is told that it was Prince Hal and Poins who had robbed him at Gadshill:

FAUKENBRIDGE: I knew thee, Mall, now, by my sword I knew thee.

FALSTAFF: By the Lord, I knew ye as well as he that made ye.

Also, as Mrs. Lancashire further points out, the Prince John of LAY strongly resembles Hotspur in 1 HENRY IV, both in the way he and his brother quarrel of land in sc. ii, just as Hotspur and Glendower do in 1 HENRY IV, III. i., and in his rantings and ravings at several places in LAY. It is also possible that Skinke is modeled (rather loosely) on Falstaff, though this is less certain.

Beside the specific and definite indebtedness to 1 HENRY IV, Lancashire shows that LAY also seems indebted to COMEDY OF ERRORS for certain aspects of the disguise comedy, and also for the gold-chain episode; and it is probable that KING JOHN furnished at least the idea for the Faulconbridge romantic subplot involving Prince Richard.

The completely unhistorical character Skinke seems to have been worked up partly from Falstaff, partly as a necessary foil to Gloucester, and partly to show the kind of opportunistic and ruthless characters that troubled and ungoverned times always throw up. His name means a tapster, drawer, waiter, and also a type of lizard(5), suggesting both his lower class origins and his resemblance to the chameleon, which can change its appearance as readily as Skinke does.

Robin Hood, Earl of Huntington, is almost certainly derived from THE DOWNFALL and THE DEATH OF ROBERT EARL OF HUNTINGTON, two plays of 1598 by Anthony Munday, perhaps with the collaboration of Henry Chettle(6). Since he does little of real importance which could not be done by someone not named Robin Hood, his presence was almost certainly required only as a drawing-card following the great success of the Huntington plays in what was almost certainly the previous season (see discussion of date below).

The legend of Rosamond is, in one sense, an especially important source of LOOKE ABOUT YOU, even though Rosamond never appears as a character. The first scene of the play, which sets the whole plot going, shows Skinke, Rosamond's (fictitious) murderer, being summoned to Parliament, where the party of the young king hopes to have him pardoned and rewarded for his deed.

The Rosamond legend is of course based on the historical Rosamond Clifford, daughter of Sir Walter de Clifford, and acknowledged mistress of Henry II (see DNB), and has been

thoroughly investigated   in Virgil B. Heltzel's FAIR ROSAMOND
(Evanston, 1947).

Rosamond seems to have enjoyed a particular popularity in
Elizabethan literature, since, besides the chronicles, no less
than six writers use her story in their works. She appears
under her own name in William Warner's ALBION'S ENGLAND
(London: G. Robinson, 1586; STC 25079), Ch. XLI; "A Mournefull
Dittie, on the Death of Rosamond, King Henry the second's
Concubine," in Thomas Deloney, THE GARLAND OF GOOD WILL (ent.
in SR 5 March 1593); Samuel Daniel, "The Complaint of
Rosamond," in DELIA (London, J. C[harlwood], 1592; STC 7193);
Michael Drayton, ENGLAND'S HEROICAL EPISTLES (London, J.
R[oberts], 1597; STC 7193); and in the present play.

Rosamond is also clearly the model for the character of
Angellica, the King's mistress who is murdered on the order of
his jealous queen in R. I.'s THE MOST PLEASANT HISTORY OF TOM
A LINCOLNE(7).

In LOOKE ABOUT YOU the familiar legend is present:
Rosamond becomes Henry's mistress, is kept in a house
surrounded by a maze or labyrinth (the "laborinth" of line
233), and is, despite this precaution, found out and murdered
by the jealous queen, who is thereafter punished by her
husband with imprisonment. All this has taken place by the
time LOOKE ABOUT YOU opens with Skinke's summons to the
Parliament. Skinke, in fact, is the only addition to the
legend which the play makes, for the earlier versions had the
queen kill Rosamond directly, not by means of a hired
assassin.

Beyond these main sources, there are several lines in
LOOKE ABOUT YOU which have seemed to various scholars to be
reminiscent of lines in two other Shakespeare plays of the
1590's. The first two occur in ROMEO AND JULIET (1595-96; all
quotations and dates of first production that follow are from
THE RIVERSIDE SHAKESPEARE ed. G. B. Evans [Boston, 1974]). As
Sir Edmund Chambers noted in discussing LOOKE ABOUT YOU in his
THE ELIZABETHAN STAGE (Oxford, 1923), Faukenbridge's speech
comparing his wife with his intended mistress (actually his
wife in disguise) at l. 2340-41:

FAUKENBRIDGE: ....why she is a very dowdy,
A dishclout, a foule jipsie unto thee.

is reminiscent of two different lines in R&J, the first being
Mercutio's line at II.iv.39-40:

    "Laura to his lady was a kitchen-wench"

and the second being the Nurse's line comparing Romeo with
Paris at III.v.219:

    "Romeo's a dishclout to him."

The second reminiscence is not noted in Chambers. It is the
line (116) in which Lord Leicester describes how the rumor of
Queen Elinor's imprisonment is spreading: "Ist't not more
wrong   when   her   mother   zeale / Sounded through Europe,
Affricke, Assia, /

     "Tels in the hollow of newes-thirsting eares

Queen Elinor lives in a dungion..." which seems reminiscent of
Juliet's line (III.v.2-3): "It was the nightingale, and not
the lark,/

     "That pierc'd the fearful hollow of thine ear."

     To conclude, then, the sources of LOOKE ABOUT YOU are
varied, but fall into four main categories: the chronicles,
especially Holinshed's; Shakespeare's plays (especially 1
HENRY IV, COMEDY OF ERRORS, and KING JOHN); the Huntington
plays; and the legend of Fair Rosamond.

                              STYLE

     The style of LOOKE ABOUT YOU is one of its strongest
points. The verse is excellent for the most part, and quite
varied, falling into three main divisions: the general blank
verse which most of the noble or upper-class characters speak;
rhymed iambic pentameter, which all the noble characters speak
occasionally, a favorite device being, as Mrs. Lancashire
points out (p. 99), the alternation of a rhymed couplet with a
line of blank verse; and rapid-fire, divided lines, with or
without rhyme.

     Examples of these three styles follow:

1) ROBERT: ... Hermit devout and reverend,
If drousie age keepe not thy stiffened joyntes,
On thy unrestfull bed, or if the houres
Of holy Orizons detayne thee not,
Come foorth.   (1. 10-14)

2) SKINKE: Good morrow son,
Good morrow and God blesse thee Huntington.
A brighter gleame of true Nobility
Shines not in any youth more then in thee.
Thou shalt be rich in honour, full of speed,
Thou shalt win foes by feare, and friends by meede.
                                     (1. 16-21)

3) HENRY: Why hayre-brain'd brother can yee brooke no jest?
I doe confirme you Earle of Nottingham.

JOHN: And Moorton too?

HENRY: I and Moorton too.

JOHN: Why so, now once more Ile sit downe by you.
                              (11. 284-87)

    The prose in LOOKE ABOUT YOU is also excellent, being natural and flexible, and well adapted to comic purposes, being spoken by the cynical but cheerful servant Blocke, by Redcap, by the Drawer, and by the Pursevant. Huntington sometimes speaks in prose, more often in blank verse, depending on whom he is speaking with (a handy knack for one who would later be famous for his ability to get along easily with the lower classes, as well as with his own). Skinke also speaks in both verse and prose, depending (generally) on whether he happens to be impersonating any one else or not. Redcap speaks with a stutter, which greatly enhances the comic nature of his speeches, and the speeches of those who are, from time to time, disguised as him.

    Examples of Blocke's and Redcap's prose follow:

BLOCKE: I heare say Redcaps father shall bee hanged this after noone, Ile see him slip a string though I give my service the slip; beside my Lady bad me heare his examination at his death; Ile get a good place, and pen it word for word, and as I like it, set out a mournefull Dittie to the tune of Labandalashot, or rowe wel ye Marriners, or somewhat as my muse shall me invoke.   (11. 1450-56)

REDCAP: G God a mercy, f fa faith and ever th thou co co come to the Fl Fl Fleete, Ile give the tu tu turning of the ke key f for n no nothing.   (11. 513-15)

DATE, AUTHORSHIP, PRINTING HISTORY

    Since LOOKE ABOUT YOU clearly follows, rather than precedes the Huntington plays in calling Robin Hood an Earl of Huntington, it is not likely to have beeen written before 15 February 1598, when Philip Henslowe paid Anthony Munday five pounds for the finished "play boocke"(8) of the first of the two Huntington plays, THE DOWNFALL OF ROBERT EARL OF HUNTINGTON.
    Though we have no guiding entry in the Stationers Register to fix an exact date for entry of copy, LOOKE ABOUT YOU was, on the evidence of Ferbrand's title-page, printed in 1600, which sets a terminal date of composition. Malcolm Nelson(9) and Sir Edmund Chambers(10) conclude that the play was written in late 1598 or early 1599, and the present editor agrees.

The authorship of the play is a rather more vexing question. Though no mention of LOOKE ABOUT YOU or any other play which is likely to be it is found in either the Stationers Register or Henslowe's Diary, the latter does contain the information that Henslowe "lent out unto Antony Wadeson" twenty shillings "in earnest of a boocke called the life of the humeros earlle of Gloster with his conquest of portingalle" on 13 June 1601.(11) Since LOOKE ABOUT YOU concludes with Gloucester (who has been referred to several times, including by himself, disguised as Redcap, as the "humorous Earl") planning to drive the Saracens out of Portugal, this lost play was quite possibly a sequel to LOOKE ABOUT YOU. Sir Walter Greg, who edited the Malone Society reprint of LAY (1913), concludes (p. v.) that there is some evidence therefore for supposing that Wadeson may have written LOOKE ABOUT YOU as well as its presumed sequel.

Professor Lancashire, who edited the play in modern spelling as a dissertation at Harvard in 1965, inclines to the view that either Anthony Munday or Henry Chettle, who seem to have collaborated on the Huntington plays, wrote LOOKE ABOUT YOU also, basing her argument partly on structure and partly on verbal similarities.(12) The possibility of Wadeson being the author she disregards, since, although the play is lost, she thinks it "highly likely that the "Honourable Life" was not a sequel to LOOKE ABOUT YOU."(13) She believes that the play is by one author only, probably by either Munday or Chettle, "with the odds perhaps favoring Chettle,"(14) though she also lists Robert Wilson (author of THE COBBLER'S PROPHECY) and Thomas Dekker as possible alternatives. Various other writers (Golding, Fleay, Oliphant, Sykes, Jones, Jenkins, Jewkes, and Jones-Davies -- see last section of Introduction for citations) discuss these possibilities, all equally inconclusively.

The view of the present editor is that on the extant evidence the authorship of LOOKE ABOUT YOU simply cannot be determined with any degree of certainty. The play is not similar enough to the known works of Munday, Chettle, Wilson or Dekker to be ascribed to any of them on internal evidence alone, and the only external evidence, the entry in Henslowe's Diary, suggests a man who has not been survived by any known works at all. If he was the same Antony Wadeson who matriculated at age sixteen at Magdalen College, Oxford, on 15 October 1590(15), he was at least old enough to have written a play in 1598 or 1599, but that is hardly an attribution. The question of authorship must remain open.

There is only one early printing, that of William Ferbrand, London, a the "signe of the Crowne, neere Guild-hall Gate," 1600.

THE TEXT:
I. Description

This is the only early edition:

A / PLEASANT / COMMODIE / [in ital.] CALLED / Looke about you. / As it was lately played by the right honoura-/ ble the Lord High Admirall his seruaunts / [printer's device of Edward Allde, McKerrow 284] / LONDON, / Printed for Willam Ferbrand, and are to be / solde at his shop at the signe of the Crowne / neere Guild-hall Gate / 1600

The volume is a quarto, collating A-L4, 44 leaves, unpaged. Alv is blank. The verso half of the running title "A Pleasant Commody / called Looke About You." is replaced on A2v, Bv, B2v, Cv, C4v, Dv, D2v, Fv, F4v, H2v, H3v, K2v, and K3v, by the variant verso headline "A Pleasant Commody,". There are no errors in catchwords, but the following variants do occur: A3v: Old / A4 Olde; Dv: Por. God / D2: Po. God; D2: Ioh: And / D2v: Io. And; D3v: Hen. Ile / D4 He. Ile; Ev: Harke / E2: Harke,; E2v: Skin. Ile / E3: Ski. Ile; E4: Bloc. By / E4v: Blo. By; F3: Ioh. What / F3v: Io. What; G4v: Fau. Mary / H: Fa. Mary; H2: Bee/ H2v Be; K2v: Ri. Is / K3: Rich. Is.

The text is printed in roman, speech-prefixes and characters' names in italic, 38 lines to the page. Edward Allde's device (McKerrow 310) follows the text on F4v.

Eight copies are known to exist, and were collated for this edition: British Museum (pressmark c. 34. b. 32); Dyce Collection, South Kensington; Bodleian (two, pressmarks Mal. 225[5], and Vet. Al e. 96); Folger (pressmark 16799); Harvard (pressmark 14434.37.5*); Huntington; and National Library of Scotland (pressmark Bute 330). The Bodleian, Harvard, Folger and National Library of Scotland copies were examined by the present editor, and are described in note 16 below.

II. Choice of Copy-text.

There was only one early and authoritative edition. Of the eight copies of it extant, only two are perfect, the Huntington and Folger. Since the Folger copy has proved more accessible for personal examination and collation, and because of much faulty inking in the Huntington, the Folger copy has been chosen as the copy-text for this edition.

III. Printing of the Copy-text.

a. Copy

The printer's copy for the first edition of the play was almost certainly not a prompt-book, since the stage-directions, while reasonably full, do contain errors and omissions (for locations, see all stage directions within square brackets in the present edition) which could not be tolerated in a prompt-book. The text is reasonably free of cruxes and metrical problems, if not of mislineation. This suggests either an authorial fair copy, or perhaps authorial foul papers corrected by the author preliminary to the preparation of a scribal fair copy.

b. Presswork

Two sets of skeletons were used in imposing the formes. Set I, which contained the variant verso headline " A Pleasant Commody," was used in imposing sheets A-D, in both the inner and outer formes. Set II, containing four new headlines, was used in imposing sheet E, and thereafter was used in alternation with Set I.

The presence of two skeletons suggests that the volume may have been printed on two presses. This would have made it particularly convenient to have had two compositors setting up from copy. The use of single rather than double "l" in spelling words on E2v, E3, E3v, E4, Gv, G2v, H1, H3v, H4, H4v, I1v, K2v, and K3v; the use of double "e" in pronouns on B2, C1v, F2v, G1; and the spelling Anan for the more usual Anon on F1v, F2v, F3, and F3v, does suggest the possible presence of more than one compositor. But the absence of any discoverable forme pattern makes it clear that if there was a second compositor, he must merely have helped the first on certain pages. And if Mrs. Lancashire is right in supposing (p. 358), that the Anan variants are intended to suggest a distinctive manner of speech on the part of the Drawer, and we may safely discount a certain number of the single and double "e" and "l" variants as being the result of crowded or short lines, then taken on the whole, the presence of the second compositor is largely conjectural, and we must conclude that the play was quite probably set up by one compositor.

IV. Modern Editions to 1980.

William Carew Hazlitt's reprint of the play in his edition of DODSLEY'S OLD PLAYS (1876) is on the whole rather bad, being reliable neither for punctuation, nor spellings, nor for the accuracy of his accounts of some of the "variants" he claimed to have found in his "old copy," nor even for accurate substantive readings. Hazlitt is, in fact, better at emending the text than he is at reproducing it, and I have admitted a number of his emendations in my text.

Sir Walter Greg's, for the Malone Society (1913), is a diplomatic reprint, without notes, contains several errors, and misses a variant (Jh. for Joh. in a speech-prefix on Sig. B1, British Museum copy). It is a fairly good reprint, but hardly a critical edition.

Anne Charlotte Begor [Lancashire]'s excellent edition has

proved so useful, that readers of my edition must already feel quite familiar with hers. It is a completely modernized edition, possibly because of dissertation requirements, and has the copious notes and appendices that one expects in a doctoral dissertation (Harvard, 1965), but which are too expensive to include in a printed book. If it were old-spelling, and if it had been published, I would probably not have edited the play myself.

One needs an old spelling edition for essentially scholarly purposes: studies of Allde's compositors, future computer assisted authorship determination studies by means of spelling or word-length, and perhaps other studies not now even envisioned, just as compositor-determination, word-length studies, and computers were not envisioned fifty or sixty years ago.

V. A Note on the Edited Text

The text is printed in old-spelling, reproducing as accurately as possible the readings of the copy-text, and only expanding the macron and ampersand and other abbreviations, and modernizing the typography. Speech prefixes, which were printed in italics in the original, are printed in solid caps here, and are normalized, but not modernized. Original stage directions, which were printed in the copy-text in italics, are here signalled by the sign ¶, and are printed in solid caps when they occur in the same line with dialogue as an added aid in distinguishing them from speeches. Additional stage directions are enclosed in square brackets, as are one or two highly conjectural emendations.

I have numbered all lines in the text continuously, including stage directions; where a stage-direction interrupts two parts of a divided line, I have numbered all three elements as three separate lines.

In Redcap's stammerings I have capitalized the initial stammered syllables if the word itslf is capitalized, since this seems always to have been done in the original when enough upper-case letters were available.

Punctuation has been modernized only to the extent of substituting periods for commas at the ends of speeches where no interruption of the speaker is suggestd by syntax or action. I have generally not otherwise altered the punctuation except where it was clearly wrong, or so misleading that I needed to emend it in any case; all such instances are mentioned in the Textual Notes.

I have gratefully followed Greg's scene divisions and Lancashire's scene-locations, and have added these to my text in square brackets.

The Textual Notes record all changes made in this text, all variants in the eight extant copies of the original printing, and all variant emendations of other editors where I have emended a line or admitted another editor's emendation. They do not contain a complete collation of Hazlitt's peculiar scene divisions, nor of his many unnecessary emendations, nor of the supposed variants of his "old copy," nor of variants found in MS. portions of the original copies which supply missing pages, though I have considered MS. corrections in the original copies as emendations and have treated them accordingly.

The usual form of the Textual Note consists of a lemma drawn from the exact reading in the text, followed by a square bracket, the variant or other peculiarity to be recorded, and the siglum or sigla of the copy or copies involved.

For example, the note on line 511 records the variant reading ty de in the British Museum, Bodleian (Malone), and Huntington Library copies. The note therefore reads:

> 511 tyde] ty de B, Bm, Hn

Sigla recorded as Ed. are the emendations of the present editor. The emendations of previous editors are marked with the last name (in parentheses) of the editor who first proposed the emendation.

Explanatory Notes, which gloss difficult words and provide background material, immediately follow the text itself, and are keyed to it by line numbers.

MODERN PERFORMANCES

The only known performances of LOOKE ABOUT YOU since the last decade of the sixteenth century were presented by the Summer Festival Theatre and the University of Toronto Graduate Centre for the Study of Drama in Toronto, June 14-23 1977, under the direction of Jonathan Rittenhouse. No cuts were made in the text, and the show ran three hours and ten minutes, with a ten minute intermission between scenes xi and xii. A large number of men's roles were played by women (just the reverse of the Elizabethan convention), there was at least one extra curtain call, and I gather from my informants that it was a charming production.

For the convenience of future directors of LOOKE ABOUT YOU (of whom I hope there will be many), here follows the doubling table from the Toronto production, which Mr. Rittenhouse has very kindly provided:

Actor   Part(s)
  1) Old King and Watch
  2) Young King and Pursevant
  3) Prince Richard
  4) Prince John

5) Queen Elinor and Humphrey
6) Gloster, and Isabel
7) Skinke
8) Robin Hood and Drawer
9) Faukenbridge
10) Lady Faukenbridge
11) Leister amd Porter
12) Lancaster
13) Redcap
14) Blocke
15) Chester and Sheriff and Huntsman and Herald
16) Servant and Warden and Watch and Huntsman and Young
    Queen

REFERENCES

The most important works for a study of LOOKE ABOUT YOU are the following:

Bradbrook, M. C. SHAKESPEARE AND ELIZABETHAN POETRY. London: 1951.

Byrne, M. St. Clair. "Bibliographical Clues in Collaborate Plays." LIBRARY XIII (1932-33), 21-48.

Golding, S. R. "Robert Wilson and SIR THOMAS MORE." N & Q 154 (1928), 237-39.

Heltzel, V. B. FAIR ROSAMOND: A STUDY OF THE DEVELOPMENT OF A LITERARY THEME. Evanston: 1947.

Hirsch, R. S. M. "An Introduction to the Huntington Plays." Unpublished M. A. Thesis, Brown University: 1968.

Holzknecht, Karl J. "Theatrical Billposting in the Age of Elizabeth." PQ II (1923), 267-81.

Jenkins, Harold. THE LIFE AND WORKS OF HENRY CHETTLE. London: 1924.

Jewkes, W. T. ACT DIVISION IN ELIZABETHAN AND JACOBEAN PLAYS. Hamden, Conn.: 1958.

Jones, F. L. "LOOK ABOUT YOU and THE DISGUISES." PMLA, XLIV (1929), 835-41.

Jones-Davies, M. T. UN PEINTRE DE LA VIE LONDONIENNE: THOMAS DEKKER. 2 vols. Paris: 1958.

Lancashire, Anne B. "LOOK ABOUT YOU as a History Play." SEL, IX, 2 (Spring 1969), 321-34.

[Lancashire,] Anne C. B."LOOK ABOUT YOU: A Critical Edition." Unpublished dissertation, Harvard University: 1965.

Nelson, Malcolm A. "LOOK ABOUT YOU and the Robin Hood Tradition." N & Q new ser. IX, 4 (1962), 141-3.

Oliphant, E. H. C. "How not to Play the Game of Parallels." JEGP XXVIII (1929), 1-15.

Ribner, Irving. THE ENGLISH HISTORY PLAY IN THE AGE OF SHAKESPEARE. PRINCETON: 1965.

Sykes, H. D. "The Dramatic Works of Henry Chettle." N & Q

CXLIV (1923) passim.
    Wallerstein,   Ruth.   KING   JOHN   IN   FACT   AND   FICTION.
Philadelphia: 1917.

NOTES TO THE INTRODUCTION

(1) DNB s.v. Gloucester, Robert Duke of.

(2) "LOOK ABOUT YOU as a History Play," SEL, IX, 2 (Spring 1969), 332-4.

(3) The edition here quoted is that of Henry Ellis (London, 1807-8).

(4) All of which were noted first by Mrs. Lancashire, "LAY as a History Play," p. 324-5.

(5) OED, IX, 146.

(6) Malcolm A. Nelson, "LOOK ABOUT YOU and the Robin Hood Tradition," N & Q new ser. IX, 4 (April 1962), 141-43.

(7) Ed. R. S. M. Hirsch, Renaissance English Text Society, vol. 7-8,(Columbia, S. C., 1978), p. xiv.

(8) HENSLOWE'S DIARY ed. R. A. Foakes and R. T. Rickert (Cambridge, 1961), p. 86.

(9) Nelson, p. 143.

(10) THE ELIZABETHAN STAGE (Oxford, 1923), IV, p. 28, as cited in Nelson, p. 141.

(11) HENSLOWE'S DIARY, f. 87v.

(12) Anne Charlotte Begor [Lancashire], "LOOK ABOUT YOU: A Critical Edition," Unpublished dissertation, Harvard University, 1965, p. 78.

(13) Lancashire diss., p. 60.

(14) Lancashire diss., p. 78.

(15) Joseph Foster, ed., ALUMNI OXONIENSIS (Oxford, 1892), IV, p. 1552.

(16) Description of Bodleian Mal. 229 (5): Rebound 1927. Front fly-leaf has purchase note signed by E.M. [Edmund Malone]. MS. initials M. D. on title-page [M. Dutton, from whom Malone purchased it]; leaves paged in pencil, u.r.c. Average foxing. Sigs. K-L wanting, but supplied in MS. by [George] Steevens, from copy of Kemble or Duke of Roxburgh, according to E. M.

note. Last line and catchword on C1 inserted in MS., as is catchword of C3. Probable provenance: M. Dutton; Edmund Malone; Bodleian Library (1821).

Description of Bodleian Vet. al e. 96: Modern green 1/2 morocco and green buckram binding. Title wanting. Lower margins of K3 and K4 torn. Front paste-down endpaper bears bookplate of Robert Herring and MS. note: "Bt at Sotheby's sale 17/18 Dec. 1956. Lot 452." No earlier owners known.

Description of Folger Shakespeare Library 16799: Perfect. Two MS. insertions, neither in text proper: 1) altered speech-prefix on H2v; 2) added sig. K on I4. Both probably 18th Cent. Bound in 3/4 light brown calf with brown boards. Front paste-down endpaper contains plates of William Holgate and Henry Huth; front free endpaper has two notations, first certainly by William A. White: 1) W. A. White / Aug. 31, 1914; 2) Taken from Skakespeare's King John / 3 others known! / With quotations from Romeo & Juliet / and 1 Henry IV! In u.r.c of back paste-down endpaper is pencilled notation by F. S. Ferguson of Bernard Quaritch Ltd., the London booksellers: "Perfect / (Several plain margins mended / catchword on D1b cut into and / that on K3a slightly defective) / Bernard Quaritch / F. S. Ferguson / 16.vii.1914" In the l.r.c. of the same endpaper is the following notation of sale prices: "

$$£ \frac{135}{-15} \text{ Huth, BQ}$$
$$\overline{120 \text{ \& } 10\% \text{ of } 663"}$$

In u.l.c. is the probable pressmark "S.0361," in the l.r.c. the letter "C" and in the l. l. c. "B." In the center of this back paste-down endpaper is the Folger Shakespeare Library bookplate. The provenance is William Holgate; Thomas Corser (1846); Henry Huth (1869); William A. White (1914); Folger Shakespeare Library (1926).

Description of National Library of Scotland Bute 330: Bound in 1/2 green morocco and green buckram, title and date on spine. Front paste-down endpaper bears bookplate of House of Falkland. A1 (title) wanting; A2 bears MS. note:" Printed in 1600" in what is apparently an old hand and black-brown ink. Cropped close in binding. K3 missing u.r. corner. Rear paste-down endpaper bears National Library of Scotland Bute Collection bookplate. Provenance: Third Earl of Bute (1713-1792); Major Michael Crichton-Stuart (descendant of 3rd earl); National Library of Scotland (1956).

Description of Harvard University 14434.37.5* (Houghton): Old green morocco binding, mostly rubbed off to brown. Front paste-down endpaper bears bookplate: "Harvard College Library/ [Seal]/ From the Gift of Ernest Blaney Dane/ (Class of 1892)/ of Boston." Cancel fly-leaf bears MS. note:"ΔΥΧΥ Y" Hunt 1/28/20 / Clawson 468." Title-page bears MS. note: "First Edition" under Allde's device. Provenance: J. W. Dodd; J. P. Kemble (1797); Duke of Devonshire (1821); Henry E. Huntington (1914); J. L. Clawson (1918); Harvard University (1926).

A
PLEASANT
COMMODIE,
Called

Looke About
You.

[DRAMATIS PERSONAE*

KING Henry II of England
QUEENE Elinor of Aquitaine, his consort
HENRY king, crowned in his father's lifetime)
RICHARD Prince of England   )-their sons
JOHN Earl of Murton   )

GLOSTER (Robert Earl of Gloucester, kinsman to the King)

Earl of LANCASTER
Earl of CHESTER
Earl of LEICESTER
ROBERT Hood, Earl of Huntington, Prince Richard's Ward

Sir Richard FAUKENBRIDGE
LADY Marrian Faukenbridge, his wife and Gloster°s sister

SKINKE

WARDEN of the Fleet
PORTER of the Fleet
REDCAP his son
BLOCKE   )
)- servants to Faukenbridge
HUMPHREY   )
PURSEVANT
DRAWER
SHERIFF
CONSTABLE
OFFICER
PAGE to Lady Rawford
SERVANT to Robin Hood
Wife to Prince Henry
Musician(s)
Isabel, wife to Prince John, Liefetenant of the Tower, Lords,
two Heralds, Officers, Huntsmen, Surgion, Servants.]

*information on practical doubling will be found in the
section on modern performances, pp. xxiii-xxiv in the
Introduction.

Looke About You.

[A2]   ¶Enter ROBERT Hood a young Noble-man, a servant with him,
with ryding wandes in theyr handes, as if they had beene new
lighted.

ROBERT: Goe, walke the horses, wayte me on the hill,   5
This is the Hermits Cell, goe out of sight:
My busines with him must not be reveal'd,
To any mortall creature but himselfe.

SERVANT: Ile waite your honour in the crosse high-way. ¶EXIT.

ROBERT: Doe so: Hermit devout and reverend,   10
If drousie age keepe not thy stiffened joyntes,
On thy unrestfull bed, or if the houres
Of holy Orizons detayne thee not,
Come foorth.
                ¶Enter SKINKE like an Hermit.   15

SKINKE: Good morrow son,
Good morrow, and God blesse thee Huntington,
A brighter Gleame of true Nobility
Shines not in any youth more then in thee.
Thou shalt be rich in honour, full of speed,   20
Thou shalt win foes by feare, and friends by meede.

ROBERT: Father, I come not now to know my fate,
Important busines urgeth Princely Richard, ¶DELIVER LETTERS.
In these termes to salute thy reverent age.
Read and be briefe, I know some cause of trust,   25
Made him imploy me for his messenger.

SKINKE: A cause of trust indeed true honoured youth,
Princes had need in matters of import,
[A2ᵛ] To make nice choyse faire Earle, if I not erre,
Thou art the Princes ward.

ROBERT: Father I am   30
His ward, his Chamberlaine and bed-fellow.

SKINKE: Faire fall thee honourable Robert Hood,
Wend to Prince Richard, say though I am loath,
To use my skill in Conjuration:
Yet Skinke that poysoned red cheekt Rosamond,   35
Shall make appearaunce at the Parlament,
He shall be there by noone assure his Grace.

ROBERT: Good morrow Father, see you faile him not,
For though the villaine did a horrible deed,
Yet hath the young King, Richard, and Earle John,   40
Sworne to defend him from his greatest foes.

SKINKE: Gods benizon be with thee noble Earle.

ROBERT: Adew good father, holla there, my horse?   ¶EXIT.

SKINKE: Up, spur the kicking Jade, while I make speede
To Conjure Skinke out of his Hermits weede;   45
Lye there religion, keepe thy Master's grave,
And on the faire trust of these Princes word
To Court againe Skinke: but before I goe,
Let mischiefe take advise of villany,
Why to the Hermit letters should be sent,   50
To poast Skinke to the Court incontinent:
Is there no tricke in this? ha let me see?
Or doe they know already I am he?
If they doe so, faith westward then with Skinke:
But what an asse am I to be thus fond,   55
Heere lyes the Hermit whom I dying found
Some two monthes since, when I was howerly charg'd
With Hugh the Cryer and with Constables,
I saw him in the ready way to heaven,
I helpt him forward, t'was a holy deed;   60
And there he lyes some sixe foote in the ground,
Since when, and since, I kept me in his weedes.
O what a world of fooles have fill'd my Cell;
For Fortunes, run-awaies, stolne goods, lost cattle,
Among the number, all the faction   65
That take the young Kings part against the olde;
[A3]   Come to my selfe to harken for my selfe,
So did the adverse party make enquire,
But eyther fall full of contrary desire:
The olde Kings part would kill me being stain'd,   70
The young Kings keep me from their violence.
So then thou needst not feare, goe boldly on,
Brave Hall, Prince Dicke, and my spruce hot spur John,
Heer's their safe conduct: O but for Rosamond!
A fig for Rosamond, to this hope Ile leane: 75
At a Queenes bidding I did kill a queane.   [EXIT.]

[Sc. ii. Westminster.]

¶Sound Trumpets, enter with a Harrald   on   the   one   side,
[KING] Henry the second Crowned, after him LANCASTER, CHESTER,
Sir Richard FAUKENBRIDGE: on the other part, King HENRY 80
the   Sonne   crowned,   Herrald   after   him: after   him   Prince
RICHARD, JOHN, LEYSTER, being set, enters fantasticall Robert
of GLOSTER in a gowne girt: walkes up and downe.

KING: Why doth not Gloster take his honoured seate?

GLOSTER: In faith my Liege Gloster is in a land   85
Where neyther suerty is to sit or stand.
I onely doe appeare as I am summoned,
And will awaite without till I am call'd.

HENRY: Why heare you Gloster?

GLOSTER: Henry I doe heare you.

HENRY: And why not King?

GLOSTER: What's he that sits so neere you? 90

RICHARD: King too.

GLOSTER: Two Kings? ha, ha.

KING: Gloster sit we charge
                                            [thee.

GLOSTER: I will obey your charge, I will sit downe,
But in this house, on no seate but the ground.

JOHN: The seat's too good.

GLOSTER: I know it brother John.

JOHN: Thy brother?

KING: Silence there.   95

HENRY: Passe to the billes Sir Richard Faukenbridge.

FAUKENBRIDGE: My Lieges both, olde Faukenbridge is proude
Of your right honour'd charge. He that worst may
Will straine his olde eyes, God send peace this day.
[A3ᵛ] A bill for the releasement of the Queene prefer'd   100
By Henry the young King, Richard the Prince, John Earle
Of Murton, Bohmine Earle of Leister and the commons.

KING: Did you preferre this byll?

ALL: We did.

CHESTER, LANCASTER: Yee did not well.

GLOSTER: Why this is good, now shall we have the hell.   104

THREE BROTHERS: Chester and Lanchaster you wrong the King.

CHESTER, LANCASTER: Our King we doe not.

HENRY: Doe not you see mé
                               [crown'd?

LANCASTER: But whilst he lives we to none else are bound.

LEYSTER: Is it not wrong thinke you, when all the world
Troubled with rumour of a captive Queene,
Imprisoned by her husband in a Realme,   110
Where her owne sonne doth weare a Diademe?
Is like an head of people mutinous,
Still murmuring at the shame done her and us?
Is't not more wrong when her mother zeale
Sounded through Europe, Affricke, Assia,   115
Tels in the hollow of newes-thirsting eares,
Queene Elinor lives in a dungion,
For pitty and affection to her sonne:
But when the true cause, Cliffords daughters death,
Shall be exposed to stranger nations: 120
What vollumes will be writ, what lybels spred?
And in each lyne our state dishonoured.

FAUKENBRIDGE: My Lord speakes to the purpose,
Mary it may be so, pray God it proove not so.

LEYSTER: Heare me conclude, and there withall conclude,   125
It is an heynous and unheard-of sinne:
Queene Elinor daughter to Kingly Fraunce,
King Henries wife and royall Henries mother,
Is kept close prisoner for an acte of Justice,
Committed on an odious Concubine.   130

KING: Thou wrongst her Leister.

LEYSTER: Leachers ever praise
The cause of their confusion, she was vile.

FAUKENBRIDGE: She was ill spoken of it's true, true.

GLOSTER: [Aside] Yonder sits one would doe as much for you.
[A4]   Olde foole, young Richard hath a gift I know it,   135
And on your wife my sister would bestow it.
Heer's a good world men hate adulterous sin,
Count it a gulfe, and yet they needs will in.

LEYSTER: What answer for the Queene?

LANCASTER: The King replyes
Your words are foule slaunderous forgeryes.   140

JOHN: His highness sayes not so.

LANCASTER: His highness doth,

[Gesturing toward KING.]

Tels you its a shame for such wilde youth,
To smother any impiety,
With shew to chastice loose adulterie.   145
Say Rosamond was Henries Concubine,
Had never King a Concubine but he?
Did Rosamond begin the fires in Fraunce?
Made she the Northerne borders reeke with flames?
Unpeopled she the townes of Picardy?   150
Left she the wives of England husbandles?
O no: she sinn'd, I graunt, so doe we all,
She fell her selfe, desiring none should fall;
But Elinor whom you so much commend,
Hath been the bellowes of seditious fire,   155
Eyther through Jealious rage or mad desire;
Ist not a shame to thinke that she hath arm'd
Foure Sonnes right hands against their fathers head,
And not the children of a low-priz'd wretch,
But one whom God on earth hath deified?   160
See where he sits with sorrow in his eyes,
Three of his Sonnes and hers tutor'd by her,
Smiles whilst he weeps, and with a proude disdaine,
Imbrace blith mirth, while his sad heart complaine.

FAUKENBRIDGE: Ha laugh they? nay by the rood that is not
                                                    [wel,
Now fie young Princes fie.

HENRY: Peace doting foole.   166

JOHN: Be silent asse.

FAUKENBRIDGE: With all my heart my Lords,
My humble leave my Lords. Gods mother asse
And foole for speaking truth, tis terrible,
But fare yee well my Lords.   170

RICHARD: Nay stay good Faukenbridge, impute it rage,
[A4ᵛ] That thus abuses your right reverend age,
My brothers are too hot.

FAUKENBRIDGE: Too hot indeed,
Foole, asse for speaking truth? it's more than need.

RICHARD: Nay good Sir Richard at my kinde intreate   175
For all the love I beare your noble house,
Let not your absence kindle further wrath,
Each side's at counsell now sit downe I pray,
Ile quite it with the kindest love I may.

GLOSTER: [Aside] I to his wife.

FAUKENBRIDGE: Prince Richard Ile sit downe,
But by the faith I owe fayre Englands Crowne,   181
Had you not been I would have left the place,
My service merits not so much disgrace.

RICHARD: Good Faukenbridge I thanke thee.

              ¶Go to their places.   185

GLOSTER: [Aside]   And you'l thinke of
                                      [him,
If you can step into his bower at Stepney.

FAUKENBRIDGE: [Aside] Prince Richard's very kinde, I know his
                                      [kindenes,
He loves me, but he loves my Lady better,
No more, Ile watch him, Ile prevent his game,   190
Young Lad, it's ill to halt before the lame.

    ¶They breake asunder. Papers this while being offred
              and subscribed betweene eyther.

HENRY: Ile not subscribe to this indignity,
Ile not be call'd a King but be a King;   195
Allow me halfe the Realme, give me the North,
The Provinces that lye beyond the Seas,
Wales and the Isles that compasse in the mayne.

GLOSTER: Nay give him all and he will scant be pleas'd.

RICHARD: Brother you aske too much.

JOHN: Too much, too little,
Hee shall have that and more, I sweare he shall.   201
I will have Nottingham and Salisbury,
Stafford and Darby, and some other Earledome,
Or by Saint John (whose blessed name I beare)
Ile make these places like a wildernes.   205
Ist not a plague, an horrible abuse,
A King, a King of England should be Father
To foure such proper youths, as Hall, and Dicke,

[B]   My brother Geffrey and my proper selfe,
       And yet not give his sonnes such maintenaunce   210
       As he consumes among his minions.

       RICHARD: Be more respective John.

       JOHN: Respective Richard?
       Are you turned pure? a changing wether-cocke?
       I say it's reason Henry should be King,
       Thou Prince, I Duke, as Jeffrey is a Duke.   215

       LANCASTER: What shall your Father doe?

       JOHN: Live at his prayers,
       Have a sufficient pention by the yere,
       Repent his sinnes because his end is neere.

       GLOSTER: A gratious sonne, a very gratious sonne.

       KING: Will this content you? I that have sat still,   220
       Amaz'd to see my sonnes devoyde of shame;
       To heare my subjects with rebellious tongues,
       Wound the kinde bosome of their Soveraigne,
       Can no more beare, but from a bleeding hart
       Deliver all my love, for all your hate: 225
       Will this content thee cruell Elinor?
       Your savage mother, my uncivill Queene;
       The Tygresse that hath drunke the purple bloud,
       Of three times twenty thousand valiant men;
       Washing her red chaps, in the weeping teares,   230
       Of widdows, virgins, nurses, sucking babes.
       And lastly sorted with her damn'd consorts,
       Entred a laborinth to murther love.
       Will this content you? she shall be releast,
       That she may next seaze me she most envyes.   235

       HENRY: Our mothers liberty is some content.

       KING: What else would Henry have?

       HENRY: The Kingdome.

       KING: Peruse this byll, drawe neere let us conferre.

       JOHN: Hall be not answered but with Soveraignty,
       For glorious is the sway of Majesty.   240

       KING: What would content you John?

       JOHN: Five Earledomes Sir.

       KING: What you sonne Richard?

RICHARD: Pardon gratious father,
And th'furtheraunce for my vow of penance:
For I have sworne to God and all his Saints,
These armes erected in rebellious brawles,   245
Against my Father and my Soveraigne,

[B^v]   Shall fight the battles of the Lord of hoasts,
In wrong'd Judea and Palestina,
That shall be Richards pennance for his pride,
His bloud a satisfaction for his sinne,   250
His patrimony, men, munition,
And meanes to waft them into Siria.

KING: Thou shalt have thy desire, Heroyicke Sonne,
As soone as other home-bred brawles are done.

LANCASTER: Why weepes olde Faukenbridge?

FAUKENBRIDGE: I am almost blinde,
To heare sons cruell, and the fathers kinde,   256
Now well a neere that ere I liv'd to see,
Such patience and so much impiety.

GLOSTER: Brother content thee this is but the first,
Worse is a brewing and yet not the worst.   260

LEYSTER: You shall not stand to this?

HENRY: And why my Lord?

LEYSTER: The lands of Moorton doth belong to John.

HENRY: What's that to me, by Acte of Parlament,
If they be mine confirm'd, he must be pleas'd.

JOHN: Be pleas'd King puppet? have I stood for thee,   265
Even in the mouth of death? open'd my armes
To sercle in seditious ugly shape?
Shooke hands with duety, bad adew to vertue,
Prophan'd all Majesty in heaven and earth;
Writ in blacke Carracters on my white brow,   270
The name of rebell John against his Father:
For thee, for thee, thou Otimie of honour,
Thou worme of Majesty, thou froth, thou buble.
And must I now be pleas'd in pease to stand,
While statutes make thee owner of my land?   275

GLOSTER: [Aside] Good pastime good, now will the theeves fall
                                                            [out!

JOHN: O if I doe, let me be never held
Royall King Henryes sonne, pardon me father,

Pull downe this rebell that hath done thee wrong.
Dicke, come and leave his side, assayle him Lords,   280
Let's have no parly but with billes and swoordes.

KING: Peace John, lay downe thy armes, heare Henry speake,
He mindes thee no such wrong.

JOHN: He were not best.

[B2] HENRY: Why hayre-brain'd brother can yee brooke no jest?
I doe confirme you Earle of Nottingham.   285

JOHN: And Moorton too?

HENRY: I and Moorton too.

JOHN: Why so, now once more Ile sit downe by you.

GLOSTER: Blow winde, the youngest of King Henries stocke,
Would fitly serve to make a weather-cocke.

JOHN: Gape earth, challenge thine owne as Gloster lyes,   290
Pitty such mucke is cover'd with the skies.

FAUKENBRIDGE: Be quiet good my Lords, the Kings commaund
You should be quiet, and tis very meete,
It's most convenient, how say you Prince Richard?

RICHARD: It is indeed.

FAUKENBRIDGE: Why that is wisely said,   295
You are a very kinde indifferent man,
[Aside] Mary a God, and by my hollidame,
Were not I had a feeling in my head,
Of some suspition twixt my wife and him,
I should affect him more then all the world.   300

GLOSTER: Take heede olde Richard, keep thee there mad lad,
My sister's faire, and beauty may turne bad.

          ¶Enter ROBERT Hood a paper in his hand.

OFFICER: Roome there, make roome for young Huntington.

FAUKENBRIDGE: A gallant youth, a proper Gentleman.   305

HENRY: Richard I have had wrong about his wardship.

RICHARD: You cannot right your selfe.

JOHN: He can and shall.

RICHARD: Not with your help, but honourable youth
Have yee perform'd the busines I enjoyn'd?

ROBERT: I have, and Skinke is come, heere is his bill,   310

HENRY: No matter for his bill let him come in.

KING: Let him not enter, his infectious breath
Will poyson the assembly.

GLOSTER: Never doubt,
Ther's more infectious breaths about your Throne,
Leyster is there, your envious Sonnes is there;   315
If them you can endure, no poyson feare.

KING: Content thee Gloster.

GLOSTER: I must be content,
When you that should mend all are patient.

                [Enter SKINKE.]

HENRY: Welcome good Skinke thou justly dost complaine,   320
Thou standst in dread of death for Rosamond,
[B2ᵛ] Whom thou didst poyson at our dread commaund,
And the appointment of our gratious Mother;
See heere my Fathers hand unto thy pardon.

SKINKE: I receive it gratiously, wishing his soule sweet
peace, in heaven for so meritorious a worke, for I feare me I
have not his heart though his hand.   327

KING: Be sure thou hast not, murderous bloud-sucker,
To jealious envy executioner.

HENRY: Besides thou suest to have some maintenaunce,   330
We have bethought us how wee will reward thee,
Thou shalt have Rowden Lordship.

GLOSTER: Shall he so?
Will you reward your murtherers with my lands?

HENRY: Your lands? it is our gift and he shall have it.

GLOSTER: Ile give him seasure first with this and this.   335

                ¶Strike him.

JOHN: Lay holde on Gloster.

KING: Hold that murtherous Skinke.

GLOSTER: Villaines hands off, I am a Prince, a Peere,
And I have borne disgrace while I can beare.

FAUKENBRIDGE: Knaves leave your rudenes, how now brother
                                              [Gloster?
Nay be appeas'd, be patient brother.   341

RICHARD: Shift for thyself good Skinke, ther's golde, away:
Heere will be parts.

SKINKE: Swonds Ile make one and stay.

JOHN: I prethee be gone since thus it falleth out,
Take water, hence, away, thy life I doubt.   345

SKINKE: Well, farewell, get I once out of doore,
Skinke never will put trust in warrants more.   ¶EXIT.

KING: Will Gloster not be bridled?

GLOSTER: Yes my Liege
And sadled too, and ryd, and spur'd, and rayn'd, ·
Such misery (in your Raigne) falles your friends,   350
Let goe my armes, you dunghyls let me speake.

KING: Wher's that knave Skinke? I charge you see him stayd.

FAUKENBRIDGE: The swift heel'd knave is fled, body a mee
Heer's rule, heer's worke indeed.

KING: Follow that Skinke, let privy search be made,   355
Let not one passe except he be well knowne,
Let poastes be every way sent speedily,
For ten miles compasse round about the Citty.

[B3]   HENRY: Take Gloster to you Liefetenant of the Tower,
Keep him aside till we conferre a while,   360
Father you must subscribe to his committing.

LANCASTER: Why must he Henry?

LEYSTER: Mary for this cause,
He hath broke peace and violated lawes.

GLOSTER: So have you all done, rebels as you be.

FAUKENBRIDGE: Good words good brother, heare me gratious
                                              [Lords,

HENRY: I prethee Faukenbridge be patient,   366
Gloster must of force answere this contempt.

KING: I will not yeeld he shall unto the Tower,
Warden of th' Fleete take you the charge of Gloster.

HENRY: Why be it so, yet stay with him a while,   370
Till we take order for the company
That shall attend him, and resort to him.

GLOSTER: Warden of the Fleete I see I am your charge,
Befriend me thus, least by theyr commaund,
I be prevented of what I intend.   375

WARDEN: Commaund me any service in my power.

GLOSTER: I pray you call some nimble footed fellow,
To doe a message for me to my sister.

WARDEN: Call in Redcap, he waiteth with a Tipstaffe,

                    ¶Exit one for him.   380

He stammers, but he's swift and trusty Sir.

                    ¶Enter REDCAP.

GLOSTER: No matter for his stammering, is this he?

REDCAP: I I am am Re Redcap s s sir.

GLOSTER: Run Redcap to Stepney.   385

REDCAP: Ile be at Stepney p p presently.   [HE BEGINS TO RUN.]

GLOSTER: Nay stay, goe to the Lady Faukenbridge my sister.

                [REDCAP continues to run.]

REDCAP: The La La Lady Fau Fau Faukenbreech, I r r run sir.

                [He continues running.]   390

GLOSTER: But take thy errand, tell her I am prisoner,
Committed to the Fleete.

REDCAP: I am g g glad of th th that, my fa fa father the   p   p
porter sha shall ge ge get a f f fee by you.   ¶STILL RUNNES.

GLOSTER: Stand still a while, desire her to make meanes   395
Unto Prince Richard for my liberty,
At thy returne (make speed) I will reward thee.

REDCAP: I am g g gone si sir.   [EXIT, RUNNING.]

RICHARD: Commend me to her gentle Huntington,
[B3ᵛ] Tell her in these affayres Ile stand her friend,   400
Her brother shall not long be prisoner:
Say I will visit her immediatlie.
Be gone sweete boy to Marian Faukenbridge,
Thou lookest like love perswade her to be loving.

ROBERT: So farre as honour will I will perswade,   405
Ile lay loves battery to her modest eares,
Second my milde assault, you may chaunce win,
Fare parley at the least, may hap passe in.   ¶EXIT.

HENRY: Heere take your charge, let no man speake with him,
Except our selfe, our brethren, or Earle Leicester.   410

FAUKENBRIDGE: Not I my Lord, may not I speake with him?

HENRY: Yes Faukenbridge thou shalt.

JOHN: And why? he is
His wives brother.

FAUKENBRIDGE: Earle John, although I be,
1 am true unto the State, and so is he.

GLOSTER: What, shal I have no servant of my owne?   415

HENRY: No, but the houshold servants of the Fleete.

GLOSTER: I thanke you kinsman King, your father knowes,
Gloster may boldelie give a base slave blowes.

FAUKENBRIDGE: O but not heere, it was not well done heere.

KING: Farewell good Gloster, you shall heere from us.   420

GLOSTER: Even what your Sonnes will suffer you to send;
Ist not a miserie to see you stand,
That sometime was, the Monarch of this land,
Intreating traytors for a subjects freedome?

LEYSTER: Let him not speake, away with him to prison.   425

GLOSTER: Heer's like to be a well stayd common wealth,
Where in proude Leister, and licentious John,
Are pillers for the King to leane upon.

JOHN: Wee'l heare your rayling Lecture in the Fleete.

HENRY: On our displeasure see he speake no more.   430

GLOSTER: On thy displeasure, well yee have me heere;

O that I were within my Fort of Bungye
Whose walles are washt with the cleare streames of Waveney,
Then would not Gloster passe a halfe-penny,
For all these rebels, and their poore King too.   435
Laughst thou King Henry? thou knows my words are true,
God help thee good olde man, adew, adew.

[Exeunt GLOSTER and WARDEN.]

[B4]   JOHN: That Castle shall be mine, where stands it
                                    [Faukenbridge?

FAUKENBRIDGE: Far from your reach sure, under Feckhill ridge,
Five hundred men (England hath few such wight)   441
Keeps it for Glosters use both day and night:
But you may easily winne it, wantons words
Quickly can master men, tongues out brawle swords.

JOHN: Yee are an Idyot.

RICHARD: I prethee John forbeare.   445

JOHN: What shall olde winter with his frosty jestes,
Crosse flowry pleasure?

FAUKENBRIDGE: I and nip you too,
God mary mother I would tickle you
Were there no more in place but I and you.

KING: Sease these contentions, forward to the Tower,   450
Release Queene Elinor, and leave me there
Your prisoner I am sure, if yee had power,
Ther's nothing lets you but the commons feare:
Keep your State Lords, we will by water goe,
Making the Fresh Thames, salt with teares of woe.   455

HENRY: And wee'll by land through the Citty ride,
Making the people tremble at our pride.

¶Exeunt with Trumpets two waies.

[Sc. iii. Fields East of London.]
¶Enter SKINKE solus.   460

SKINKE: Blacke Heath quoth he, and I were King of all Kent, I
would give it for a commodity of Apron-strings, to be in my
cottage agen. Princes warrants, mary Skinke findes them as
sure as an obligation seal'd with butter. At Kings Bridge I
durst not enter a boate, through London the stones were   465
fiery, I have had a good coole way through the fieldes, and in
the high way to Ratcliffe stands a heater: Mile-end's covered

with Who goes there. Tis for me sure; O Kent, O Kent, I would
give my part of all Christendome to feele thee as I see thee.
If I goe forward I am stayed, if I goe backward, ther's a 470
roge in a red cap, he's run from Saint Johnes after me: I were
best stay heere, least if he come with hue and cry, he stop me
yonder, I would slip the coller for feare of the halter; but
heere comes my runner, and if he run for me, his race dyes, he

[B4ᵛ]   is as sure dead, as if a Parlament/of Devils had decreed it.

¶Enter REDCAP.   476

REDCAP: Ste Ste Stepney chi church yonder, but I have forgot
The La La Lady Fau Fau Fau plague on her, I mu must b backe to
the Fle Fle Fleete to kn kn know it. The La the La La Fau,
plague on't; GGloster will goe ne neere to st stab me, fo 480
for forgetting my errand, he is such a ma ma mad Lord, the La
Lady Fau Fau Fau.

SKINKE: Help me devise, upon my life this foole is sent
From Gloster to his sister Marian.

REDCAP: I m must nee needs goe backe, the La Lady Fau Fau 485
Fau.

SKINKE: God speed good fellow.

REDCAP: Go go god sp sp speed you sir.

SKINKE: Why run'st thou from me?

REDCAP: Ma mary sir, I have lo lost a La Ladyes name, and 490
am running ba backe to se se seeke it.

SKINKE: What Lady I prethee stay.

REDCAP: Why the La Lady Fau Fau Fau.

SKINKE: Faukenbridge?

REDCAP: I the s s same, f f farewell, I th thanke you hartily

SKINKE: If thou wouldst speake with her she is in Kent,   496
I serve her, what's thy busines with my Lady?

REDCAP: I sh sh should doe an errand to her f f from my Lord
of Gloster, but a a and she be in K Kent, Ile s send it by
you.   500

SKINKE: Where is my Lord?

REDCAP: Mary p p prisoner in the Fl Fleete, a a and a w would
have her speake to P Prince R Richard for his re re release.

SKINKE: I have much busines, hold ther's thy fare by water, my
Lady lyes this night   505

REDCAP: Wh Wh Where I pray?

SKINKE: At Gravesend at the Angell.

REDCAP: Tis devillish co co colde going by water.

SKINKE: Why ther's my cloake and hat to keepe thee warme,
Thy cap and Jerkin will serve me to ride in   510
By the way, thou hast winde and tyde, take Oares.
[C]   My Lady will reward thee royally.

REDCAP: G God a mercy, f fa faith and ever th thou co co come
to the Fl Fl Fleete, Ile give the tu tu turning of the ke key
f for n no nothing.   515

SKINKE: Hye thee, to morrow morning at Graves-end Ile wash thy
stammering throate with a mug of ale merrily.

REDCAP: God be w with you till s soo soone; what call you the
Lady? O now I re remember the La Lady Fa Faukenbridge at what
s signe?   520

SKINKE: At the Angell.

REDCAP: A Angell, the La La Lady Fa Fa Faukenbridge, Fa   Fau
Faukenbridge.

                          [EXIT.]

SKINKE: Farewell and bee hang'd good stammering ninny, I 525
thinke I have set your Redcaps heeles   a running, wold your
Pyanet chattering humour could as sa safely se set mee fr from
the searchers walkes. Yonder comes some one, hem: Skinke   to
your   trickes this tytty tytty a the tongue I beleeve will
faile mee.   530

               ¶Enter CONSTABLE and Watch.

CONSTABLE: Come make up to this fellow, let th'other go, he
seems a gentleman, what are you sir?

SKINKE: [Aside] Would I had kept my owne sute, if the
countenaunce carry it away.   535

CONSTABLE: Stand sirra, what are you?

SKINKE: The Po Po Porters Sonne of the F Fl Fleete, going to
Stepney about businesse to the La La Lady Fa Fa Faukenbridge.

CONSTABLE: Well bring him thether, some two or three of yee
honest neyghbors, and so backe to the Fleete, we'll shew   540
ourselves dilligent above other Officers.

SKINKE: Wh wh why le le let me run I am Re Redcap.

CONSTABLE: Well, sure you shall now run no faster than I lead
you, heare yee neighbor Simmes, I leave my staffe with yee,
bee vigilent I pray you, search the suspitious houses at the
townes end, this Skink's a trouncer; come, will you be gone
sir?   547

SKINKE: Yes sir, [Aside] and the devill goe with you and them,
well, yet have hope mad ha hart, co co come your way.

                    ¶Exeunt.   550

                    [Sc. iv. Stepney.]
                ¶Enters ROBERT Hood and BLOCKE.

[Cᵛ]   BLOCKE: Sweet nobilitie in reversion, Blocke by the commission
of his head, Conjures you and withall bindes you, by all the
tricks that pages passe in time of Parlament, as swearing 555
to the pantable, crowning with Custords, paper whiffes to the
sleepers noses, cutting of tagges, stealing of torches, CUM
MULTIS ALIIS, tell Blocke, what Blocke you have cast in the
way of my Ladies content.

ROBERT: Block by the antiquity of your ancestrie, I have 560
given your lady not so much as the least cause of dislike, if
she be despleased at any newes I bring, it's more then I must
blab.

BLOCKE: Zounds these pages be so proude, they care not for an
olde Servingman, you are a ward and so, an Earle, and no 565
more: you disquiet our house that's the most: and I may be
even with thee that's the least.

                ¶Enter the LADIE Faukenbridge.

LADY: What Blocke, what Blocke I say what doe you there?

BLOCKE: Making the young Lord merry Maddame,   570

LADY: Go attend ye gate, see if you can let in more greife
therat,

BLOCKE: Zounds and greife come in there, and I see him once
Ile conjure his gaberdine.

LADY: Will you be gone sir?   575

BLOCKE: [Aside] Hem, these women, these women, and she bee not
in love eyther with Prince Richard or this lad, let Blocks
head be made a chopping blocke.   ¶EXIT BLOCKE.

ROBERT: Faire madam, what replye you to my sute,
The prince expects smiles, welcomes, loving lookes,   580

LADY: The Prince, if he give heed to Marrians sute,
Must heare heart-sigh's, see sorrow in my eyes,
And finde cold welcome to calamities,

ROBERT: And why for gods sake?

LADY: Even for Glosters sake,

ROBERT: Why by mine honnor, and Prince Richards faith,   585
Your brother Gloster shall have liberty,
Uppon condition you release a prisoner
That you have longe held in captivitye.

LADY: I have no prisoner,

ROBERT: Yes a world of eies,
Your beuty in a willing bondage ties   590

LADY: Go to, you are dispos'd to jest my Lord,

[C2]   ROBERT: In earnest I must be an earnest suter
To you for love, yet you must be my tuter.

LADY: Are you in love?

ROBERT: I dearely love Prince Richard.

LADY: Then doe you love the loveliest man alive.   595
The Princeliest person of King Henries sonnes,

ROBERT: I like this well.

LADY: He is vertuous in his minde, his body faire,
His deeds are Just, his speaches debonaire,

ROBERT: Better and better still.   600

LADY: In deed he is what no body can denye,
All lovely, beautie all, all Majestie.

ROBERT: Ile tel his excelence what you reporte,
No doubt he will be very thankfull, for't,

LADY: Nay heare you young Lord? Gods pitty stay.   605

ROBERT: What have you more in Richards praise to say?

LADY: I have said to much if you misconster me.
Dutie bids praise him, not unchastitie.

ROBERT: Unchastitie holy heavens forfend it,
That he or I, or you should once intend it,   610

               ¶Enter BLOCKE and RICHARD.

BLOCKE: They are there sir, close at it, I leave you sir, the
more roome the lesse company.

RICHARD: Drinke that, farwell.   614

BLOCKE: If that sir Richard comes, this ties, this bindes,
O golde, thy power converteth servants mindes.   ¶EXIT.

RICHARD: How now faire Maddam who hath angred you?

LADY: Greife at my brothers duraunce angers me.

RICHARD: I had thought my Ward young Huntington had vext you.

LADY: Who he? alas good Gentleman he wrong'd me not.   620
[Aside] No matter for all this, Ile tell your tale.

          ¶A noyse within, Enter SKINKE, BLOCKE, CONSTABLE.

BLOCKE: Sir there comes no more of you in with him then the
Constable. Zounds heares a beadroll of Billes at the gate
indeed, back ye base   625

LADY: Now sirra whats the matter?

BLOCKE: Marry heares a stammerer taken clipping the Kings
English, and the Constable and his watch hath brought him to
you to be examin'd.   629

[C2ᵛ] CONSTABLE: No Madam wee are commaunded by the King to watch,
and meeting this fellow at Mile-end, he tels us, he is the
Porters sonne of the Fleete, that the Earle of Gloster sent
him to you.

SKINKE: I f f forsooth h he desire you to speake to the p
Prince for him.   635

LADY: O I conceave thee, bid him blithly fare,
Beare him this Ring in token of my care.

SKINKE: [Aside] If I be rid of this evill Angell   that   haunts
mee, many rings, much Fleete will Skinke come unto.   639

CONSTABLE: Madam, if you know this fellow we'll discharge him.

BLOCKE: Madam,   and   you be wise, trust your honest neighbors
heere, let them bring this ca ca ca ca to the Fleete, and   s
see your ring delivered.

SKINKE: [Aside] A plague upon you for a damned roge,
The Porter of the Fleete will surely know me.   645

LADY: Good neighbors bring this honest fellow thether,
Ther's for his paines a crowne, if he say true,
And for your labour ther's as much for you.

SKINKE: Why Ma Ma Madam, I am Re Re Redcap the Porters sonne.

LADY: Thou hast no wrong in this farewell good fellow.   650

SKINkE: [Aside] Best speaking to Prince Richard? no Ile try
And face out Redcap if the slave were by.

LADY: Make them drinke Blocke.

BLOCKE: Come to the Buttery bar, stitty stitty stammerer, come
honest Constable, hey the watch of our towne, we'll drinke
trylill I faith.   656

     ¶As they goe out, enters Sir Richard FAUKENBRIDGE
          stealing forward, Prince and LADY talking.

ROBERT: LUPUS IN FABULA my Noble Lord,
See the olde foxe Sir Richard Faukenbridge.   660

RICHARD: We'll fit him well enough, second us Robin.

LADY: [Aside] Ile fit you well enough for all your hope.

          ¶FAUKENBRIDGE beckens to BLOCKE.

FAUKENBRIDGE: Leave quaffing sirra, listen to their talke.

BLOCKE: O while you live beware, two are sooner seene then
one: 666
          Besides beare a braine Master,
          If Blocke should be now spide,
          My Madam would not trust this sconce
[C3]   Neither in/time nor tyde.   670

FAUKENBRIDGE: Well, leave me, now it buds; see see, they
                                                  [kisse.

BLOCKE: Adew good olde sinner, you may recover it with a
sallet of parsley, and the hearbe patience, if not sir you
knowe the worst, it's but even this.   [EXIT.]   675

RICHARD: Madam, what you desire I not deny,
But promise Glosters life and liberty,
I beg but love.

FAUKENBRIDGE: When doth she give her almes?

LADY: Faire honourable Prince.

FAUKENBRIDGE: Nay then they speed.

LADY: My soule hath your deserts in good esteeme.   680

FAUKENBRIDGE: Witnesse these goodly tines that grace my head.

LADY: But were you the sole Monarch of the earth,
Your power were insufficient to invade,
My never yeelding heart of chastity.

FAUKENBRIDGE: Sayst thou so Mall, I promise thee for this,
Ile owe thy cherry lips an olde mans kisse;   686
Looke how my Cockerill droopes, tis no matter,
I like it best when women will not flatter.

RICHARD: Nay but sweet Lady.

ROBERT: Nay but gracious Lord,
Doe not so much forget your Princely worth,   690
As to attempt vertue to unchastity.

FAUKENBRIDGE: O noble youth!

ROBERT: Let not the Ladies dead greife for her brother,
Give life to shamelesse and detested sinne.

FAUKENBRIDGE: Sweet childe.   695

ROBERT: Consider that she is of high decent.

FAUKENBRIDGE: Most vertuous Earle.

ROBERT: Wife to the noblest Knight that ever breath'd.

FAUKENBRIDGE: Now blessing on thee blessed Huntington.

ROBERT: And would you then first staine your Princely stocke,
Wrong beauty, vertue, honor, chastitye,   701
And blemmish Faukenbridges untaynted armes?

FAUKENBRIDGE: By adding hornes unto our Falcones head,
Well thought on noble youth, twas well put in.

LADY: Besides my gratious Lord,

[C3ᵛ] FAUKENBRIDGE: Tickle him Mall,   705
Plague him on that side for his hot desire.

LADY: How ever secretly great Princes sin,

FAUKENBRIDGE: Oh now the spring she'll do it secretly.

LADY: The King of all harts will have all syns knowne.

FAUKENBRIDGE: Ah then she yeilds not.

RICHARD: Lady heer's my hand, 710
I did but try your honorable faith.

FAUKENBRIDGE: He did but trie her, would she have bin tride
It had gone hard on this and on this side.

RICHARD: And since I see your vertue so confirm'd,
As vice can have no entraunce in your heart,   715
I vow in sight of heaven never againe,
To moove like question but for love,

FAUKENBRIDGE: My heart is eased, holde Blocke take up my
                                        ⌊cloake.

BLOCKE: And your cap to sir.

RICHARD: Sir Richard?

FAUKENBRIDGE: What sweet Prince welcome yfaith,   720
I see youth quickly gets the starte of age;
But welcome welcome and young Huntington.
Sweet Robyn Hude, honors best flowring bloome,
Welcome to Faukenbridge with all my hearte,
How cheares my love, how fares my Marrian, ha?   725
Be merry chucke, and Prince Richard welcome,
[Aside to LADY] Let it goe Mall I knowe thy grevances.
Away away, tut let it passe sweet girle,
Wee needs must have his helpe about the Earle.

LADY: Let it not be delayd deere Faukenbridge.   730

RICHARD: Sir Richard, first make sute unto my father,
Ile follow you to Courte and second you,

FAUKENBRIDGE: [Aside] Follow to Court, ha? then I smell a
                                        ⌊rat,

Its probable he'll have about agayne,
Long seige makes entrance to the strongest fort,   735
It must not be I must not leave him heere,
[To Richard] Prince Richard, if you love my brothers good,
Lets ride backe to the Courte, Ile wayte on you.

RICHARD: [Aside] He's Jelious, but I must observe the tyme,
We'll ride unto the Court, Ile leave my boy   740
Till we returne, are you agreed to this?

[C4]   FAUKENBRIDGE: Oh hee is an honourable youth.
Vertuous and modest, Huntingtons right heyre.
His father Gilbert was the smoothst fac't Lord
That ere bare Armes in England or in Fraunce.   745

RICHARD: Solicite Robin, Lady give good eare,
And of your brothers freedome never feare.

FAUKENBRIDGE: Marrian farwell, wheres Blocke? open the gate,
Come Prince God send us to prove fortunate?   ¶EXEUNT.

LADY: Why doe you stay sir?

ROBERT: Madam as a   750
Lidger to solicite for your absent love.

LADY: Walk in the Garden I will follow you,
Ifaith Ifaith you are a noble wagge.

ROBERT: An honorable wag, and wagish Earle.
Even what you will sweet Lady I must beare,   755
Hoping of patience, profit will ensue.
That you will beare the Prince as I beare you.

LADY: Well said well said, Ile have these toyes amended,
Goe, will you walke into the Garden sir,

ROBERT: But will you promise me to bring no maides,   760
To set upon my little manship there?
You threatned whipping, and I am in feare,

LADY: Uppon my word Ile bring none but my selfe.

ROBERT: You see I am weapned, doe not I beseech yee,
Ile stab them come there twenty ere they breech mee.   ¶EXIT.

LADY: This youth and Richard, think me easily wonne,   766
But Marrian rather will embrace,
The bony carcasse of dismaying death,
Than prove unchast to Noble Faukenbridge.
Richard's king Henries sonne, is light,   770
Wanton and loves not humble modestie,

Which makes me (much contrary to my thoughts)
Flatter his humor for my brothers safetye,
But I protest Ile dwel among the dead,
Ere I pollute my sacred nuptiall bed.   ¶EXIT.   775

[Sc. v. The Fleet Prison.]
¶Enter GLOSTER in his gowne, calling.

GLOSTER: Porter what Porter wher's this drowsie asse?

¶Enter PORTER.

PORTER: Who calles? my Lord of Gloster all alone?   780

[C4ᵛ] GLOSTER: Alone and have your wisdomes companie,
Pray wher's the stammering chatterer your sonne?
He's ever running but he makes small haste,
Ile bring his lyther legges in better frame,
And if he serve me thus another time.   ¶KNOCKE WITHIN.
Harke sir your clients knocke, and't be your pye,   786
Let him vouchsafe to chatter us some newes,
Tell him we daunce attendance in our chamber.   ¶EXIT PORTER.
This John and Henry are so full of hate,
That they will have my head by some device,   790
Gloster hath plotted meanes for an escape,
And if it fadge, why so; if not, then well,
The way to heaven is death, this life's a hell.

¶Enter PORTER and SKINKE.

PORTER: Why should the Watchmen come along with thee?   795

SKINKE: Ther's such a que question for yon s same r rogue
Skink p plague keepe me farre enough from him, that a an
honest f fellow ca cannot w w walke the streetes.

PORTER: Well sir dispatch your busines with the Earle,
He's angry at your stay I tel ye that.   ¶EXIT.   800

SKINKE: [Aside] Sbloud what a frowne this Gloster castes at
                                                    [me,
I hope he meanes to lend me no more cuffes,
Such as he paide me at the Parlament.

GLOSTER: What mutter you, what tydings from my sister?

SKINKE: Co commendations and s she hath s sent ye this r   805
ring.

GLOSTER: Hold ther's two Angels, shut the chamber doore,
You must about some busines for me strayght;

Come nearer man,

SKINKE: I feare I am to neare,

GLOSTER: Hast thou no tydings for my liberty?   810

SKINKE: No b but ye sh shall he heare f from her p p
presently.

GLOSTER: And p presently sir off with your coate.
Nay quicke, uncase, I am bold to borrow it,
Ile leave my gowne, change is no robbery.   815
Stutterer it's so, neare flinch, ye cannot passe,
Cry, and by heaven Ile cut thy cowards throate,
Quickly cashyre your selfe, you see me staye,

SKINKE: N n nay, b b but wh wh what m meane ye?

[D]   GLOSTER: To scape I hope, sir with your priviledge,   820
How now, who's this, my fine familliar Skinke?
Queene Beldam's minnion,

SKINKE: Zounds you see 'tis I.

GLOSTER: Tyme sortes not now to know these misteries.
How thou camst by this ring, or stol'st this coate,
They are mine now in possession, for which kindenes   825
If I escape Ile get thee Libertie,
Or fire the fleete about the Wardens eares,
Mumbudgit not a word as thou lovest thy life,

SKINKE: I mum mum faire, pray God may chaunce it,
My Lord, but that my state is desperate,   830
Ide see your eyes out eare I would be cheated.

GLOSTER: Walke like an Earle villaine some are comming.

                    ¶Enter JOHN and PORTER.

JOHN: Where is this Gloster?

GLOSTER: Y y yonder he walks. Fa fa father, l let me out. 835

PORTER: Why whether must you now?

GLOSTER: To Je Jericho I th thinke, tis such a h h humorous
Earle.

PORTER: Well sir wilt please you hasten home againe?

GLOSTER: I Ile be h heare in a trice; b but p praye have   840
ca care of th this madcap, if he g give us the s s slip, s s

some   of   us   a are like to m make a sl sl slyppery occupation
on't.

      ¶This while JOHN walkes and stalkes by SKINKE,
           never a word betweene them.   845

PORTER: Looke to your busines sir let me alone.

GLOSTER: [Aside] Alone? never trust me if I trouble thee.

JOHN: Mad Gloster mute, all mirth turn'd to dispaire?
Why now you see what tis to crosse a King,
Deale against Princes of the Royall blood,   850
Youle snarle and rayle, but now your toung is bedry'd,
Come caper hay, set all at six and seaven,
What musest thou with thought of hell or heaven✠

SKINKE: Of neither John I muse at my disgrace,
That I am thus kept prisoner in this place.   855

JOHN: O sir, a number are here prisoners,
My Cousen Moorton whome I came to visite,
But he good man is at his morrow masse,
[D^v] But I that neither care to say nor sing,
Come to seeke that preaching hate and prayer,   860
And while they mumble up their Orisons,
We'll play a game at bowles, what saist thou Gloster?

SKINKE: I care not if I doe,

JOHN: You doe not care,
Let olde men care for graves, we for our sportes,
Off with your gowne, there lies my hatt and Cloake,   865
The bowles there quickly, hoe?

SKINKE: No my gowne stirres not, it keeps sorrowe warme,
And she, and I am not to be devorced,

      ¶Enter PORTER with bowles.

JOHN: Yes ther's an axe must part your head and you,   870
And with your head, sorrowe will leave your heart.
But come shall I begin? a pound a game,

      [JOHN throws the Jack.]

SKINKE: More pounds and we thus heavy? well begin.

JOHN: Rub rub rub rub.   [JOHN bowls.]   875

SKINKE: Amen God send it short enough, [Aside] and mee
A safe running with them clothes from thee.

JOHN: Play Robin,   [SKINKE bowls.]   run run run.

SKINKE: Far enough and well, flye one foote more,
[Aside] Would I were halfe so far without the doore.   880

    [JOHN and SKINKE retrieve their bowls and Jack.]

    ¶Enter PORTER.

JOHN: Now Porter whats the newes?   [Throws Jack.]

PORTER: Your Coossen Moorton humbly craves,
Leaving your game, you would come visit him,   885

JOHN: Bowle Gloster Ile come presently.   [EXIT PORTER.]

    [SKINKE bowls.]

So neere mad Robin? then have after you,

    [JOHN bowls.]

SKINKE: [Aside] Would I were gone, make after as you may, 890

JOHN: Well sir tis yours, one all, throw but the Jacke
While I goe talke with Moorton: Ile not stay,
Keepe Cloake and hat in pawne Ile hould out play,

SKINKE: I would be sory John but you should stay,
Untill my bias run another way,   [EXIT JOHN.]   895
Now passe, and hey passe, Skink unto your tricks,

    [He throws off Gloster's gown.]

Tis but a chaunce at hazard: there lyes Gloster,
And heare stands Skinke, now John play thou thy part,

    [He puts on John's hat and cloake.]   900

And if I scape Ile love thee with my heart.
So. Porter let me foorth.

    ¶Enter PORTER.

[D2]   PORTER: God blesse your grace,
Ye spoke with the Lord Moorton?

SKINKE: I have   905
And must about his busines to the Courte.
It greeves me to break my sporte with Gloster,
The melancholy Earle is comfortlesse.

PORTER: I wold your grace would comfort him from hence,
The Fleet is weary of his company,   ¶REDCAP KNOCKS.   910

SKINKE: Drinke that, some knockes, I prethee let me out.
His head shall off ere long, never make doubt.   ¶EXEUNT.

            ¶Enter JOHN at the other doore.

JOHN: Now madcap thou winst all, wher art thou Robyn?
Uncased: nay then he meanes to play in earnest.   915
But whers my Cloake, my rapier and my hatt?
I holde my birth-right to a beggers scrip,
The basterd is escaped in my cloathes.
Tis well, he left me his to walke the streets,
Ile fire the Citty but Ile finde him out,   920
Perchaunce he hides himselfe to try my spleene,
Ile to his chamber, Gloster? hallo Gloster?   ¶EXIT.

            ¶Enter PORTER and REDCAP.

PORTER: I wonder how thou camst so strangly chang'd?
Tis not an hower since thou wents from hence,   925

REDCAP: By my Ch Ch Christendome I ha have not b b been h
heere this three nights, a p p plage of him, that made me such
a   ch   chaunting, and s sent me such a Ja Ja Jaunt, blud I was
st stayd for Skinke, that ill fa fa fac'd rogue.

PORTER: I pray God there be no practise in this change.   930
Now I remember these are Skinkes cloathes,
That he wore last day, at the Parlament,

    ¶Knocke, Enter at another doore, JOHN in Glosters gowne.

JOHN: Porter? you Porter?

PORTER: Doe you not heare them knock, you must stay sir,   935

JOHN: Bloud I could eate these rogues.

REDCAP: Wh Wh what raw, tis a very harsh mo morsell, ne   next
your he heart

JOHN: A plague upon your Jaunts, what porter slave?

REDCAP: I have been at g gravesend sir.   940

JOHN: What's that to me?

REDCAP: And at Ca Ca Canterbury.

[D2ᵛ] JOHN: And at the gallows: zounds this frets my soule.

REDCAP: But I c could not f finde your s s sister the La Lady
Fau Faukenbridge.   945

JOHN: You stammering slave hence, chat among your Dawes,
Come ye to mad me? while the rogue your father

¶Enter PORTER.

REDCAP: My f fa father.

JOHN: Porter? you damned slave.   950

PORTER: Ist Midsomer doe you begin to rave?

JOHN: Harke how the traytor flouts me to my teeth.
I would intreat your knaveship let me forth,
For feare I dash your branes out with the keyes,
What is become of Gloster and my garments?   955

PORTER: Alas in your apparrell Glosters gone,
I let him out even now; I am undone,

JOHN: It was your practise, and to keepe me backe
You sent Jacke Daw your sonne with ca ca ca,
To tell a sleveles tale: lay hould on him,   960
To Newgate with him! And you tut atut,
Run redcap and trudge about,
Or bid your fathers portership farwell. ¶EXEUNT WITH PORTER.

REDCAP: He heares a go good Je Je Jest by the L Lord to mo
mocke an ape withall: my fa fa father has brought his ho   965
ho hoges to a fa fa faire mmmarket. Po po Porter quoth you? p
p porter that will for me, and I po po porter it, let them   po
po post me to heaven in this qua quarter. But I must s s seeke
this Gl Gl Gloster and Sk Sk Skinke that co cony catching   ra
ra rascall, a pa pa plauge co co confound him, Re re redcap
must ru run he cannot tell whe whether.   ¶EXIT.   971

[Sc. vi. Westminster.]
¶Sound Trumpets, Enter HENRY the younger, on one hand
of him QUEENE Elinor, on the other LEYCESTER.

HENRY: Mother and Leycester adde not oyle to fire.   975
Wrath's kindled with a word, and cannot heare
The numberlesse perswasions you inhort,

QUEENE: O but my sonne thy father favours him.
Richard that vile abortive changling brat,
And Faukenbridge, are fallen at Henries feete.   980

[D3] They wooe for him, but I intreate my sonne
      Gloster may dye for this that he hath done.

      LEYSTER: If Gloster live thou wilt be overthrowne.

      QUEENE: If Gloster live thy mother dies in moane,

      LEYSTER: If Gloster live Leyster will flie the realme,   985

      QUEENE: If Gloster live thy kingdome's but a dreame.

      HENRY: Have I not sworne by that eternall arme
      That puts just vengeance sword in Monarcks hands,
      Gloster shall die for his presumption?
      What needs more conjuration gratious Mother?   990
      And honorable Leyster marke my words.
      I have a Bedrole of some threescore Lords,
      Of Glosters faction.

      QUEENE: Nay of Henries faction.
      Of thy false fathers faction, speake the truth,
      He is the head of factions; were he downe: 995
      Peace, plenty, glory will impale thy crowne.

      LEYSTER: I ther's the But; whose hart-white if we hit,
      The game is our's. Well we may rage and rove,
      At Gloster, Lancaster, Chester, Faukenbridge,
      But he is the upshot.

      QUEENE: Yet begin with Gloster.   1000

      HENRY: The destenies run to the booke of Fates,
      And read in never-changing Characters
      Robert of Glosters end, he dies today,
      So fate, so heaven, so doth King Henry say.

      QUEENE: Emperially resolv'd.   ¶TRUMPETS FAR OFF.

      LEYSTER: The olde King comes.   1005

      QUEENE: Then comes Luxurious lust,
      The King of Concubines, the King that scornes
      The undefiled, chast and nuptiall bed,
      The King that hath his Queene Imprisoned.
      For my sake scorne him, sonne call him not father,   1010
      Give him the stile of a competitor,

      HENRY: Pride seaze uppon my heart, wrath fill myne eyes,
      Sit lawfull majestie uppon my front
      Dutie flie from me, pitty bee exild,
      Sences forget that I am Henries child.   1015

[D3ᵛ] QUEENE: I kisse thee, and I blesse thee, for this thought.

¶Enter KING, LANCASTER, RICHARD, FAUKENBRIDGE.

KING: O Lancaster bid Henry yeeld some reason
Why he desires so much the death of Gloster,

HENRY: I heare thee Henry, and I thus reply.   1020
I doe desire the death of Basterd Gloster,
For that he spends the Treasure of the Crowne.
I doe desire the death of basterd Gloster,
For that he doth desire to pull me downe.
Or were this false (I purpose to be plaine)   1025
He loves thee, and for that I him disdaine.

KING: Therin thou shewest a hate-corrupted mynde,
To him the more unjust, to me unkynd.

QUEENE: He loves you as his father lov'd his mother.

KING: Fie, fie upon thee hatefull Elinor.   1030
I thought thou hadst been long since scarlet dyde,

HENRY: She is and therefore cannot change her colour.

RICHARD: You are to strickt, Earle Glosters fault
Merrits not death,

FAUKENBRIDGE: By th'rood the Prince saies true.
Heere is a statute from the Confessor,   1035

HENRY: The Confessor was but a simple foole.
Away with bookes my word shall be a lawe,
England her breath shall from this bosome drawe,
Gloster shall die,

LEYSTER: Let Gloster dye the death.

LANCASTER: Leyster he shall not,   1040
He shall have lawe, dispight of him and thee.

HENRY: What lawe, will you be Traitors? whats the lawe?

LANCASTER: His right handes losse, and that is such a losse,
As England may lament, all Christians weepe.
That hand hath bin advanst against the Moores,   1045
Driven out the Sarasins from Gads and Cicile,
Fought fifteene Battels under Christs red crosse,
And is it not (thinke you) a greevious losse,
That for a slave (and for no other harme)
It should be sundred from his Princely Arme?   1050

FAUKENBRIDGE: More for example Noble Lancaster,
But tis great pitty, to to great a pittie.

[D4]   HENRY: Ile have his hand and head.

RICHARD: Thou shalt have mine then.

QUEENE: Wel sayd stubberne Dicke, Jack wold not serve me so,
Were the boy heere: 1055

RICHARD: Both John and I have serv'd your will too long;
Mother repent your cruelty and wrong:
Gloster you know is full of mirth and glee,
And never else did your grace injury.   1059

QUEENE: Gloster shall dye.

HENRY: Fetch him heere Ile see him dead.

RICHARD: He that sturs for him shall lay downe his head.

FAUKENBRIDGE: O quiet good my Lords, patience I pray,
I thinke he comes unsent for by my fay.

                 ¶Enter JOHN in Glosters gowne.

RICHARD: What meanst thou Gloster?

HENRY: Who brought Gloster
                                 [hyther?   1065

JOHN: Let Gloster hang and them that [brought him hyther.]
There lyes his case, a mischiefe on his carkasse.

QUEENE: My deare sonne Jacke?

JOHN: Your deere son Jack an apes,
Your monkey, your babone, your asse, your gull.   1069

LEYSTER: What ayles Earle John?

JOHN: Hence, further from my sight,
My fiery thoughts and wrath have worke in hand;
Ile curse ye blacker then the Levarnian Lake,
If you stand wondering at my sorrow thus;
I am with childe, big, hugely swolne with rage,
Who'll play the Midwife, and my throbs aswage?   1075

KING: I will my Sonne.

HENRY: I will high harted brother.

JOHN: You will, and you, tut, tut all you are nothing,
Twill out, twill out, my selfe my selfe can ease:
You chafe, you swell, ye are commaunding King,
My father is your footestoole when ye please,   1080
Your word's a law, these Lords dare never speake,
Gloster must dye, your enemies must fall.

HENRY: What meanes our brother?

JOHN: He meanes that thou art mad,
She franticke, Leyster foolish, I the babe,
These grinde us, bite us, vexe us, charge, and discharge,
Gloster, O Gloster!

QUEENE: Where is Gloster sonne?   1086

HENRY: Where is Gloster brother?

KING: I hope he be escaped.

JOHN: O I could teare my hayre,
And falling thus upon the solide earth,
Dig into Glosters grave, so he were dead   1090
And gone into the depth of under worlds.
[D4^V] Or get seditions hundreth thousand hands,
And like Briareus, battle with the Starres,
To pull him downe from heaven if he were there.

FAUKENBRIDGE: Looke to Earle John the Gentleman is mad.   1095

JOHN: O who would not be mad at this disgrace?
Gloster the fox is fled, there lies his case,
He cousned me out of myne, the porter helpt him,

HENRY: The porter shall be hangd let's part and seeke him,
Gloster shall dye all Europe shall not save him.   1100

JOHN: He is wise, too wise for us, yet Ile goe with you,
To get more fooles into my company.

QUEENE: This is your fathers plot, revenge it sonne.

HENRY: Father by heaven if this were your advice,
Your head or heart shall pay the bitter price.   1105
Come mother, Brother, Leyster, let's away.

JOHN: I, Ile be one, in hope to meet the basterd,
And then no more my selfe will be his headsman.   ¶EXEUNT.

KING: Richard and Faukenbridge follow the search,
You may prevent mischaunce by meeting Gloster,   1110
If ye finde Skinke see that you apprehend him,

I heare there is a wizard at blacke heath,
Let some enquire of him where Skinke remaynes.
Although I trust not to those fallacies,
Yet now and then such men proove Soothsayers.   1115
Will you be gone?

FAUKENBRIDGE: Withall my heart, withall my heart my Lord.
Come Princely Richard, we are ever yoak'd.
Pray God there be no mistery in this,

RICHARD: Be not suspitious where there is no cause,   1120

FAUKENBRIDGE: Nay nothing, nothing, I am but in jest.

                    ¶EXEUNT.

KING: Call in a Pursevant.

LANCASTER: Heares one my Leidge.

KING: There is a porter likely to be hangd,
For letting Gloster scape, sirra attend,
You shall have a repreive to bring him us,   1125
These boys are to to stubborne Lancaster,
But tis theyr mothers fault, if thus she move me,
Ile have her head though all the world reprove me.   ¶EXEUNTT.

                    [Sc. vii. Stepney.]   1130
[E]   ¶Enter ROBERT Hood and LADY Faukenbridge.

LADY: Doe not deny me gentle Huntington.

ROBERT: My Lord will misse me.

LADY: Tut let me excuse thee.

ROBERT: Turne woman, O it is intollerable!
Except you promise me to play the Page: 1135
Doe that, try one night, and you'll laugh for ever,
To heare the Orizons that Lovers use;
Their ceremonious sighes, their idle oathes,
To heare how you are prais'd and pray'd unto.
For you are Richards Saint, they talke of Mary   1140
The blessed Virgin, but upon his beades
He onely prayes to Marrian Faukenbridge.

LADY: The more his error, but will you agree
To be the Lady Faukenbridge one day?

ROBERT: When ist?

LADY: On Munday.

ROBERT: Wherefore ist?

LADY: Nay then   1145
You doe me wrong with inquisition.
And yet I care not greatly if I tell thee.
Thou seest my husband full of jealousie;
Prince Richard in his sute importunate,
My brother Gloster threatned by young Henry;   1150
To cleare these doubtes, I will in some disguise,
Goe to blacke Heath unto the holy Hermit,
Whose wisedome in fore-telling things to come,
Will let me see the issue of my cares.
If destinyes ordaine me happines,   1155
Ile chase these mistes of sorrow from my heart,
With the bright Sunne of mirth: if fate agree,
It, and my frends, must suffer misery,
Yet Ile be merry too, till mischeefe come.
Onely I long to knowe the worst of ill.   1160

ROBERT: Ile once put on a scarlet countenaunce.

LADY: Be wary least ye be discovered Robyn.

ROBERT: Best paint me then, be sure I shall not blush.

        ¶Enter BLOCK bleeding, GLOSTER with him.

BLOCKE: Beate an Officer, Redcap Ile have ye talkt withall,
[Eᵛ] beate Sir Richards Porter? help Madam, help,   1166

GLOSTER: Peace, you damned rogue.

LADY: Brother I pray you forbeare.

GLOSTER: Zwonds a hundreth at my heales almost,
And yet the villaine stands on complaiment.

BLOCKE: A bots on you, ist you?   1170

GLOSTER: Will you to the doore you foole? and bar the gate,
Holde ther's an angell for your broaken pate;
If any knocke let them not in in haste.

BLOCKE: Well Ile doe as I see cause,
  Blood thou art deare   1175
  To me, but heere's
  A soveraigne plaister for the sore:
  Golde healeth wounds,
  Golde healeth heartes:
  What can a man have more?   ¶EXIT. 1180

LADY: Deare brother, tell us how you made escape?

GLOSTER: You see I am heare, but if you would knowe how:
I cannot scape and tell the manner too,
By this I knowe your howse is compassed
With hel-hound search.

LADY: Brother Ile furnish you   1185
With beard and hayre, and garments like my husband,
How like you that?   ¶EXIT LADY.

GLOSTER: Well, when I have them:
Quickly then dispatch: sblood turne gray beard and hayre?
Robyn conceale, this dyeteth my minde,
Myrth is the object of my humorous spleane,   1190
Thou high commaunding furie! further device,
Jests are conceated, I long to see their birth,
What come ye sister? Robyn a theeves hand,
But prethee where hadst thou this beard and haire?

LADY: Prince Richard wore them hether in a maske,   1195

GLOSTER: Saist thou me so, faith love the Princely youth,
Tut you must tast stolne pleasure now and than,

ROBERT: But if she steale and Jelious eyes espie:
She will be sure condemnd of Burglary.

GLOSTER: Ha crake? can your low stumps venter so deep   1200
Into affections streame? go to you wanton,
What want we now? my nightcap, O tis heare,
So now no Gloster, but olde Faukenbridge,
[E2]   Harke, the search knockes, ile let them in my selfe;
Welcome good fellowe; ha, what ist you lacke?   1205

            ¶Enter REDCAP with [CONSTABLE and] another.

REDCAP: Ma master Co constable, se se search you th that way,
a and you ho honest man th that way. Ile ru run th this way m
my owne se selfe.   ¶THEY DISPEARSE THEMSELVES.

GLOSTER: What search you for? what is it you would have? 1210

            ¶Enter BLOCKE.

BLOCKE: Madam, what shall I doe to these browne-bill fellowes?
some runne into the wine seller, some heere, some there.

GLOSTER: Let them alone, let them search their filles.

BLOCKE: Ile looke to their fingers for all that.   1215

GLOSTER: Doe so good Blocke, be carefull honest Blocke.

BLOCKE: Sir stammerer and your wa watch, y'are pa past
ifaith.   ¶EXIT.

GLOSTER: Will you not speake knaves, tel me who you seeke?

REDCAP: Ma mary sir we s seeke a va va vacabond, a fu   1220
fugitive, my La Ladies owne b brother; but and hee were the po
po Popes owne b brother, I would s search f f for him; for I
have a p poore father r ready to be ha ha hang'd f f for him.

GLOSTER: O tis for Gloster! mary search a gods name,
Seeke peace, will he breake prison too?   1225
It's a pitty he should live, nay I defye him.
Come looke about, search every little corner,
My selfe will lead the way, pray you come,
Seeke, seeke, and spare not, though it be labour lost:
He comes not under my roofe, heare ye wife,   1230
He comes not hyther, take it for a warning.

REDCAP: You sp sp speake like an honest ge ge Gentleman, re re
rest you me me mery, co co come my f f friends, I be beleeve h
h he r ran by the g g garden w wall toward the wa water side.

                    ¶Exeunt running.   1235

GLOSTER: This fellow is of the humour I would chuse my wife,
few words and many paces, a word and away,
    And so must I: Sister adieu,
    Pray you for me, Ile do the like for you.
    Robin farewell, commend me to the Prince.   1240

LADY: Can ye not stay heere safe?

[E2ᵛ] GLOSTER: No, Ile not trust
The changing humours of olde Faukenbridge,
Adieu yong Earle, Sister lets kisse and part;
Tush, neere mourne, I have a merry hart.   ¶EXIT.

LADY: Farewell all comfort.

ROBERT: What weeping Lady?   1245
Then I perceive you have forgot Blacke-heath.

LADY: No, there Ile learne both of his life and death.

ROBERT: Till Munday Madam I must take my leave.

LADY: You will not misse then:

ROBERT: Nay, if Robin faile yee,
Let him have never favour of faire Lady.   1250

LADY: Meane while Ile spend my time in prayers and teares,
That Gloster may escape these threatned feares.   ¶EXIT.

                    [Sc. viii. Streets of London.]
                    ¶Enter SKINKE like Prince John.

SKINKE: Thus jets my noble Skinke along the streetes,   1255
To whom each bonnet vailes, and all knees bend;
And yet my noble humour is too light,
By the sixe shillings: heere are two crackt groates
To helter skelter, at some vawting house.

              [Enter FAUKENBRIDGE at another door.]   1260

But who comes yonder? ha, olde Faukenbridge?
Hath a brave chaine, were John and he good friends,
That chaine were mine, and should unto Black-heath.
Ile venture, it's but a tryal, lucke may fall.
Good morrow good sir Richard Faukenbridge.   1265

FAUKENBRIDGE: Good morrow my sweet Prince, harty good morrow.
This greeting wel becomes us, marry does it;
Better iwis then strife and Jangling.
Now can I love ye, wil ye to the Shiriffes?
Your brother Richard hath beene there this houre.   1270

SKINKE: Yes I am plodding forward as you doe;
What cost your chaine? it's passing strongly wrought,
I would my Golde-smith had a patterne of it.

FAUKENBRIDGE: Tis at your graces service, shew it him.

SKINKE: Then dare ye trust me?

FAUKENBRIDGE: Who the Princely John?   1275
My Soveraignes sonne, why what a question's that?
Ile leave you, yee may know I dare trust you.

[E3] SKINKE: Ile bring't ye to the Shiriffes, excuse my absence.

FAUKENBRIDGE: I wil my noble Lord, adieu sweet Prince. ¶EXIT.

SKINKE: Why so, this breakfast was wel fed upon,   1280
When Skinkes devises on Blacke heath doo faile,
This and such cheates, would set me under saile,
Ile to the water side, would it were later,
For stil I am afraide to meete Prince John.

¶Enter GLOSTER like Faukenbridge.   1285

But what a mischiefe meant Faukenbridge
To come againe so soone? that way he went,
And now comes peaking; upon my life
The buzzard hath me in suspition,
But whatsoever chaunce, Ile filch a share.   1290

GLOSTER: Yonder's Prince John I hope he cannot know me,
Ther's naught but Gloster Gloster in their mouthes;
I am halfe strangled with the Garlicke breath,
Of rascals that exclaimes as I passe by,
Gloster is fled, once taken he must dye.   1295
But Ile to John, how does my gratious Lord?
What tattles rumour now? what newes of Gloster?

SKINKE: What newes could I heare since you left me last?
Were you not heere even now? lent me your chaine,
I think you dote.

GLOSTER: Sweet Prince, age, age forgets,   1300
[Aside] My brothers chaine? a pretty accident,
Ile have't and't be but in the spight of John.

   [SKINKE measures off part of the chaine with his hands.]

SKINKE:[Aside] Ther's more, and more, Ile geld it ere it goe.

           ¶He breakes the chaine.   1305

This same shal keep me in some Taverne merry,
Til nights blacke hand curtaine this to cleare sky.

GLOSTER: My sweet Prince, I have some cause to use my chaine;
Another time (when ere your Lordship please)
Tis at your service, o mary God it is.   1310

SKINKE: Heere palsie, take your chaine, stoop and be hang'd,
[Aside] Yet the fish nibled, when she might not swallow;
Gout I have curtall'd what I could not borrow.   ¶EXIT.

GLOSTER: He's gone away in frets, would he might meete
My brother Faukenbridge in this mad moode,   1315
There would be rare adoe; Why this fits me,
My braine flowes with fresh wit and pollicy.

           [Enter JOHN, RICHARD and the Sheriff.]

[E3ᵛ] But Gloster looke about, who have we yonder?
       Another John, Prince Richard and the Shiriffe?   1320
       Upon my life, the slave that had the chaine,
       Was Skinke, escapt the Fleete by some mad sleight,

Wel, farewel he, better and better still,
These seeke for me, yet I wil have my will.

JOHN: Shiriffe, in any case be diligent.   1325
Whose yonder, Faukenbridge?

GLOSTER: How now, sweet chucke,
How fares my lovely Prince?

JOHN: What carest thou?
Or well, or ill, we crave no help of thee.

GLOSTER: Gods mother doe you scorne me?

JOHN: Gout, what then?

RICHARD: Fye, leave these idle braules, I prethee John   1330
Lets follow that we are injoyn'd unto.

GLOSTER: I mary Prince, if now you slip the time,
Gloster will slip away; tut though he hate me
I have done service, I have found him out.

RICHARD: A shame confound thee for thy treachery,   1335
Inconstant dotard, tymerous olde asse,
That shakes with cowardise not with yeares.

GLOSTER: Goe, I have found him, I have winded him.

JOHN: O let me hug thee gentle Faukenbridge,
Forgive my oft ill using of thine age,   1340
Ile call thee Father, ile be penitent,
Bring me where Gloster is Ile be thy slave,
All that is mine, thou in reward shalt have.

GLOSTER: Soft, not too hasty, I would not be seene in't,
Mary a god my wife would chide me dead,   1345
If Gloster by my meanes should loose his head.
Princely Richard at this corner make your stand:
[Aside to Richard] And for I know you love my sister well,
Know I am Gloster and not Faukenbridge.   1349

RICHARD: [Aside] Heaven prosper thee sweet Prince in thy
                                        [escape.

GLOSTER: Shiriffe, make this your quarter, make good guard.
John, stay you heere, this way hee meanes to turne,
By Thomas I lacke a swoord, body a me.

JOHN: What wouldst thou with a swoord olde Faukenbridge?

GLOSTER: O sir to make shew in his defence,   1355

[E4] For I have left him yonder at a house
      A friends of mine, an honest Cittizen.

      JOHN: Wee'll fetch him thence.

      GLOSTER: Nay then you injure me,
      Stay till he come; he's in a russet cloake
      And must attend me like a Servingman.   1360

      JOHN: Holde ther's my swoord, and with my swoord my heart,
      Bring him for Godsake, and for thy desert,
      My brother King and mother Queene shall love thee.

      GLOSTER: Marke me good Prince, yonder away we come,
      I goe afore and Gloster followes me;   1365
      Let not the Shiriffe nor Richard meddle with us,
      Begin you first, seaze Gloster and arrest him;
      Ile draw and lay about me heere and heere,
      Bee heedfull that your watchmen hurt me not,

      JOHN: Ile hang him that doth hurt thee, prethee away,   1370
      I love thee but thou kilst me with delay.

      GLOSTER: Wel keep close watch, ile bring him presently.

      JOHN: Away then quickly.

      GLOSTER: Close master Shiriffe, Prince Richard,

      RICHARD: [Aside to GLOSTER]   Gloster adieu.

      GLOSTER: I trust you.

      RICHARD: By my Knighthood Ile proove true. 1375

                    ¶Exit GLOSTER.

      JOHN: Revenge, Ile build a Temple to your name;
      And the first offring shal be Glosters head,
      Thy Alters shal be sprinkled with the bloud,
      Whose wanton current his mad humour fed;   1380
      He was a rymer and a Ridler,
      A scoffer at my mother, prays'd my father,
      Ile fit him now for al, escape and all.

      RICHARD: Take heede spight burst not in his proper gall.

                    ¶Enter FAUKENBRIDGE and BLOCKE.   1385

      JOHN: How now, what way tooke Faukenbridge I wonder?
      That is not Gloster sure that attends on him.

FAUKENBRIDGE: He came not at the Shiriffes by the morrow
[masse,
I sought the Goldsmithes rowe and found him not;
Sirra, y'are sure he sent not home my chaine?   1390

BLOCKE: Who should send your chaine sir?

FAUKENBRIDGE: The Prince, Prince John: I lent it him to day.

JOHN: What's this they talke?

[E4^V] BLOCKE: By my truth Sir, and ye lent it him, I thinke   1394
you may goe look [for] it: for one of the Drawers of the
Salutation tolde me even now, that he had tooke up   a   chamber
there till evening, and then he will away to Kent.

FAUKENBRIDGE: Body of me, he meanes to spend my chaine,
Come Blocke Ile to him.

JOHN: Heare you Faukenbridge?

FAUKENBRIDGE: Why what a knave art thou? younders Prince
[John. 1400

BLOCKE: Then the Drawer's a knave, he tolde me Prince John was
at the Salutation.

JOHN: Wheres Gloster Faukenbridge?

FAUKENBRIDGE: Sweet Prince I knowe not.

JOHN: Come, jest not with me, tell me where he is?

FAUKENBRIDGE: I never saw him since the Parlament.   1405

JOHN: Impudent lyar, didst thou not even now
Say thou woldst fetch him? hadst thou not my sword?

FAUKENBRIDGE: Wert thou a King, I will not beare the lye,
Thy sword? no boy, thou seest this sword is myne.

BLOCKE: My master a lyer? Zounds wert thou a potentate,   1410

FAUKENBRIDGE: I scorne to weare thy armes untutred childe,
I fetch thee Gloster? shamelesse, did I see thee
Since, as I went this morning to the Shiriffes,
Thou borrowedst my gold chaine?

JOHN: Thy chaine?

FAUKENBRIDGE: I hope you will not cheate me princkocks John.

JOHN: Ile cheate thee of thy life if thou charge me   1416
With any chaine.

FAUKENBRIDGE: Come, let him come I pray,
Ile whip yee boy, Ile teach you to out face.

BLOCKE: Come, come, come, but one at once, ye dasterds come

RICHARD: Keepe the Kings peace, I see you are both deceav'd,
He that was last heare, was not Faukenbridge.   1421

FAUKENBRIDGE: They slaunder me, who sayes that I was heare?

RICHARD: Wee doe beleeve ye sir; nor doe you thinke
My brother John deceiv'd you of a chayne.

FAUKENBRIDGE: He did, I did deliver it with this hand.   1425

JOHN: Ile dye upon the slanderer,

FAUKENBRIDGE: Let the boy come.

[F]   BLOCKE: I, let him come, let him come.

RICHARD: Fellow, thou spakst even now, as if Prince John
Had byn at some olde Taverne in the towne.

BLOCKE: I sir, I came up now, but from the Salutation,   1430
and   a   drawer that doth not use to lye,   tolde me Prince John
hath byn there all this after noone.

JOHN: The Devill in my likenesse then is there.

FAUKENBRIDGE: The Devill in thy likenesse or thy selfe,
Had my gold chaine.

JOHN: Thou art the Devill, for thou   1435
Hadst my good sword, all these can witnesse it.

FAUKENBRIDGE: Gods Mother thou bely'st mee.

JOHN: Give me the lye?

RICHARD: Nay calme this fury, lets downe to the Taverne,
Or one, or both, these counterfeites are there.

FAUKENBRIDGE: I know him well enough that had my chaine, 1440
And there be two Johns, if I finde one there,
Ber Lady, I will lay him fast.

RICHARD: It is this Skinke that mockes us I beleeve.

JOHN: Alas poore Skink it is the Devill Gloster;
Who if I be so happy once to finde,   1445
Ile give contentment, to his troubled minde.

RICHARD: I hope he's far enough, and free enough:
Yet these conceytes I knowe delight his soule.

FAUKENBRIDGE: Followe me Blocke, follow me honest Blocke.

BLOCKE: Much follow you, I have another peece of worke 1450
in hand; I heare say Redcaps father shall bee hanged this
after noone, Ile see him slip a string though I give my
service the slip; beside my Lady bad me heare his examination
at his death: Ile get a good place, and pen it word for word,
and as I like it, set out a moornefull Dittie to the   1455
tune of Labandalashot, or rowe wel ye Marriners, or somewhat
as my muse shall me invoke.   ¶EXIT.

[Sc. ix. The Salutation Tavern.]
¶Enter GLOSTER like Faukenbridge with a PURSEVANT,
GLOSTER having a paper in his hand, the PURSEVANT bare.

GLOSTER: A charytable deed, God blesse the King,   1461
He shall be then repreeved.

PURSEVANT: I sir, some day or two, till the young King and
[F^v]   Prince /John chaunge it, especially if the good Earle bee not
found which God forbid.   1465

GLOSTER: What house is this that wee are stept into
To read this warrant in?

PURSEVANT: A Taverne sir, the Salutation.

GLOSTER: A Taverne? then I will turne prodigall,
Call for a pint of Sacke good fellow.   1470

PURSEVANT: Drawer?

DRAWER: [Within] Anan sir.

[Enter DRAWER.]

GLOSTER: A pint of thy best Sacke my pretty youth.

DRAWER: God blesse your worship sir, ye shall have the   1475
best in London sir.

GLOSTER: What knowst thou me? knowst old Faukenbridge?
I am no Taverne hunter I can tell thee.

DRAWER: But my Master hath taken many a faire pound of your
man Blocke; he was heere to day sir, and fild two bottles of
nippitate sacke.   1481

GLOSTER: Well, fill us of your nippitate sir,
This is well chauncst, but heere ye boy?
Bring Suger in white paper, not in browne;
[Aside] For in white paper I have heere a tricke,   1485
Shall make the Pursevant first swound, then sicke.
Thou honest fellow what's thy name?

PURSEVANT: My name is Winterborne sir.

GLOSTER: What countryman I prethee?

PURSEVANT: Barkeshire and please ye.   1490

GLOSTER: How long hast thou bin sworne a messenger?

PURSEVANT: But yesterday and please your worship, this is the
First imployment I have had.

                ¶Enter DRAWER with wine and Suger.

GLOSTER: A good beginning, heere have too thee fellow;   1495
Thou art my fellow now thou servest the King,
Nay take Suger too, Gods Lady deere,
I put it in my pocket, but it's heere:
Drinke a good draught I prethee Winterborne.

                ¶He drinkes and falles over the stoole.   1500

DRAWER: O Lord Sir Richard, the man, the man.

GLOSTER: What a forgetfull beast am I? peace boy,
[F2]   It is his fashion ever when he drinkes.
Fellow he hath the falling sickenes,
Run fetch two cushions to rayse up his head,   1505
And bring a little Key to ope his teeth   ¶EXIT DRAWER.
Pursevant, your warrant and your boxe,
These must with me, the shape of Faukenbridge
Will holde no longer water heere about.
Gloster wil be a proteus every houre,   1510
That Elinor and Leyster, Henry, John,
And all that rabble of hate loving curres,
May minister me more mirth to play upon.

                ¶Enter DRAWER.

DRAWER: Heer's a key sir, and one of our folke to help.   1515

GLOSTER: No matter for a key, help him but in,

And lay him by the fire a little while,
He'll wake immediatly, but be hart sicke;
Ther's money for a candle and thy wine,
Ile goe but up unto your Aldermans,   1520
And come downe presently to comfort him.   ¶EXEUNT.

[Within] SKINKE: Drawer? what Drawer? with a vengeance Drawer.

[Within] DRAWER: Speake in the Crowne there.

                    ¶Enter SKINKE like Prince John.

SKINKE: They be come, the devill crowne yee one by one,   1525
Skinke tho'art betraide, that master Faukenbridge
Missing some of his chaine, hath got thee dog'd.
Drawer? what Drawer?

DRAWER: Anan, anan sir.

SKINKE: Was not sir Richard Faukenbridge below?   1530

DRAWER: Yes and please yee.

SKINKE: It does not please me wel,
Knowes he that I am heer?

DRAWER: No I protest.

SKINKE: Come hether sirra, I have little money,
But ther's some few linkes of a chayne of golde:
Upon your honesty knowes not sir Richard,   1535
That I am heere?

DRAWER: No by my holydam.

SKINKE: Who's that was with him?

DRAWER: Why a Pursevant.

[F2ᵛ] SKINKE: Where is sir Richard?

DRAWER: At the Aldermans.

SKINKE: [Thinking] A Pursevant and at the Aldermans.
What Pyg, or Goose, or Capon have you kill'd,   1540
Within your Kitchin new?

DRAWER: A pyg new stickt.

SKINKE: Fetch me a sawcer of the bloud, quicke run;   ¶EXIT.
Ile fit the Pursevant, and Alderman,
And Faukenbridge, if Skinke have any wit.

Well Gloster, I did never love thee yet,   1545
But th'art the maddest Lord that ere I met,
If I scape this, and meete thee once againe,
Cursse Skinke, if he dye penny in thy det.

          ¶Enter DRAWER [with saucer of blood].

DRAWER: O my Lord the house is full of holberts, and a 1550
great many Gentlemen aske for the roome where Prince John is?

SKINKE: Lend me thy Aprone, runne and fetch a pot
From the next roome.

               [Exit DRAWER.]

               Betray'd, swounds betray'd, by   1555
Gout, by palsie, by dropsie;

               [Enter DRAWER.]

                    O brave boy,
Excellent bloud: up, take my cloake and my
Hat to thy share, when I come from Kent, ile   1560
Pay thee like a King.

     [SKINKE covers himself with blood, takes the pot]

DRAWER: I thanke you my Lord.   ¶EXIT.

          ¶Enter JOHN, RICHARD, FAUKENBRIDGE,
               Shiriffes and Officers.   1565

SKINKE: [Aside] Now fortune help or never: they come, [As if
to someone offstage] and yee were a Prince as yee say ye are,
yee would bee ashamed to abuse a poore servant thus, but and
if you were not of the bloud Royall, Ide breake the necke of
yee downe the stayres, so would I, Ide teach you to hurt
prentises.   1570

RICHARD: Who hurt thee fellow?

SKINKE: Prince devill or his dam, Prince John they call him.

JOHN: Gloster I hope.

RICHARD: I doubt not but it's Skinke.

JOHN: Where is he?

SKINKE: Up them stayres, take heede of him. He's in the   1575
Crowne.

FAUKENBRIDGE: Alas poore fellow, he hath crown'd thee
                                              [shrewdly.

[F3]
JOHN: In recompense, if it be him I seeke,
Ile give thee his whole head to tread upon.
Follow me brother, come olde Faukenbridge,   1580
Keep the stayres Shiriffes, you see it waxeth darke,
Take heede he slip not by you.   ¶EXEUNT.

SKINKE: Hange your selves,
This darkenes shal convay me out of doors,
Ile swim the Thames, but Ile attaine Black-heath,
London farewell, curse John, rave Faukenbridge,   1585
Skinke scapes you all by twylights privyledge.   [EXIT.]

                [Sc. x. The Same.]

[Within]: Where is he? lights, bring lights, drag out that
                                              [boy.

              ¶Enter all with the boy.

JOHN: This in my cloke, my hat, my rapier,   1590
And eyther it was Skinke or Gloster.

DRAWER: I know not who twas sir, he said he was Prince John,
he tooke away my aprone and a pottle pot with him, and al to
bloudied his head and face.

FAUKENBRIDGE: We met him, by Saint Anthony, we met him. 1595

JOHN: The fire of Saint Anthony confound
This changing counterfeit whatsoever he be.

RICHARD: It makes me laugh at envious greedines,
Who feedes upon her owne harts bitternes.

JOHN: Sirra you that were borne to cry anan,   1600
What other copesmates have you in the house?

DRAWER: Sir my Maisters gesse be none of my copesmates,

JOHN: Well your gesse, can ye gesse who they be?

DRAWER: Marry heere's a pursevant, that this Gentleman sir
Richard Faukenbridge left sick even now.   1605

FAUKENBRIDGE: Marry of God dyd I, thou lying knave?

DRAWER: I am a poore boy sir, your worship may say your

pleasure, oure maides have had a foule hand with him, you said
he would be sicke: so he is with a witnesse.

JOHN: Looke about Faukenbridge, heere's worke for you,   1610
You have some evill Angell in your shape,
Goe sirra, bring us foorth that Pursevant?

                ¶Enter two leading the PURSEVANT sicke.

RICHARD: (aside) Gloster, thou wilt be too too venterous,
Thou doost delight in those odde humours so,   1615
That much I feare they'll be thy overthrowe.

PURSEVANT: O O O not too fast; O I am sicke, O very sicke.

[F3ᵛ] JOHN: What picture of the pestilence is this?

PURSEVANT: A poore man sir, a poore man sir: downe I pray yee,
I pray let me sit downe. A sir Richard, sir Richard, a   1620
good sir Richard: what have I deserv'd to be thus dealt with
all at your worships hands? a ha, ah, ah.

FAUKENBRIDGE: At my hands knave? at my hands paltry knave?

DRAWER: And I should be brought to my booke oath sir:

[Within]: What Jeffrey?   1625

DRAWER: Anan, anan.

JOHN: A plague upon your Jeffring, is your name Jeffrey?

DRAWER: I and't please you sir.

RICHARD: Why gentle Jeffrey then stay you awhile,
What can you say, if you come to your booke?   1630

DRAWER: If I bee pos'd upon a booke sir, though I be a poore
prentise, I must speake the truth, and nothing but the truth
sir.

JOHN: And what's your truth sir?

PURSEVANT: O, O my heart.   1635

DRAWER: Mary sir this Knight, this man of worship.

FAUKENBRIDGE: Well, what of me? what did my worship doe?

DRAWER: Mary ye came into the Bel, our roome next the Barre,
with this honest man as I take it.

FAUKENBRIDGE: As thou tak'st it?   1640

PURSEVANT: O sir tis too true, too true, too true O Lord.

DRAWER: And there he call'd for a pint of Sacke, as good Sacke
(Ile be pos'd upon all the bookes that ever opened and shut)
as any is in all Christendome.

FAUKENBRIDGE: Body of me, I come and call for Sacke?   1645

PURSEVANT: O ye did, ye did, ye did, O O.

JOHN: Well forward sirra.

RICHARD: [Aside] Gloster hath done this jest.

DRAWER: And you call'd then for Suger sir, as good Suger 1649
and as wholsome, as ever came in any cup of Sacke: you drunke
to this man, and you doe well God be thanked, but hee no
sooner drunke:

PURSEVANT: But I, but I, but I, O my head, O my heart.

RICHARD: I cannot chuse but smile at these conseites.

JOHN: I am mad, and yet I must laugh at Faukenbridge.   1655
Brother, looke how sir Richard actes his rage?

[F4]   FAUKENBRIDGE: I came? I call? the man is like to dye,
Practise by th'masse, practise by the marry God,
John loves me not, Prince Richard loves my wife,
I shall be charg'd heere, for a poysned knave,   1660
Practise by th'Lord, practise I see it cleare.

PURSEVANT: And more Sir Richard, O Lord O Sir Richard,

FAUKENBRIDGE: What more? what hast thou more? what practise
                                                    [more?

PURSEVANT: O my box, my box, with the Kings armes, O my box,
O my box, it cost me, O Lord every penny O, my box,   1665

RICHARD: And what of your box sir?

DRAWER: Mary sir it's lost, and tis wel knowne my Master keeps
no theeves in his house, O there was none but you and he,

FAUKENBRIDGE: O then belike thou thinkest I had his box,

PURSEVANT: O sir Richard I will not, O Lord I will not 1670
charge you for all the world, but, but, but for the warrant
the olde King signd to repreeve the Porter of the fleet, O

God, O God!

JOHN: The Porter of the Fleet, the olde king signd,

PURSEVANT: I my good Lord, oh, oh,   1675

JOHN: Is he repreived then?

PURSEVANT: No my Lord, O sir Richard tooke it from me with his
owne hand. O.

FAUKENBRIDGE: Heeres a device to bring me in contempt
With the olde King, that I ever lov'd,   1680
Princes and Shiriffe, you can witnesse with me,
That I have bin with you, this after noone,
Onely with you, with no body but you,
And now a fellow whome the King would save,
By a repreive, this fellow sayes is hang'd,   1685

JOHN: If thou hadst done it, Ide have justified it,
But Richard I conceipt this jest already,
This mad mate Skinke, this honest merry knave,
Meeting this Pursevant, and hearing tell
He had a warrant to repreeve a slave,   1690
Whome he would hang: stole it away from him.
This is sure the Jest, upon my life it is,

PURSEVANT: O but my warrant, how shall I doe? O,

RICHARD: But looke about you, hot braind brother John,
And I beleeve you'l finde it otherwise,   1695
[F4ᵛ] Gloster hath got the warrant in disguise,
And sav'd the fellow you so faine would hang.

JOHN: No, no, how say you Master Shiriffe, is he not hang'd?

SHIRIFFE: My Lord, the gibbet was set up by noone
In the olde Bayly, and I charg'd my men,   1700
If I returne not, though it were by Toarch light,
To see him executed ere they come.

JOHN: I am greedy to heare newes.

FAUKENBRIDGE: Rob'd of my chaine, out-fac'd I had a swoord,
Accus'd of poysoning, cousonage, seeking bloud?   1705
Not to be borne; it is intollerable.

RICHARD: Sir Richard, I prethee have some patience.

FAUKENBRIDGE: Ile to Blacke-heath, talke not of patience,
It is intollerable, not to be borne.

JOHN: It is intollerable not to be borne,   1710

[Enter the Shiriffe's man with the warrant.]

A warrant brother, Faukenbridge a warrant?

FAUKENBRIDGE: [Back to him] I saw no warrant, I defie you
[all.

JOHN: [Reads] A slave, a Pursevant, one winter borne.

FAUKENBRIDGE: I care not for thee that winter borne.   1715

PURSEVANT: O it is I sir, that's my warrant.

JOHN: Ist you? you rogue, you drunkerd; ye are cheated,
And we are cheated of the prisoner,
Out dog, dog.

PURSEVANT: O o o o my Lord.   ¶EXIT AND DRAWER.   1720

SHIRIFFE: Have patience and we wil have a privy search.

JOHN: Goe hang ye block-heads, get ye from my sight,
O would I were a Basiliske, to kill
These gleare ey'd villaines.

SHIRIFFE: Come away let's leave him.
We have a warrant let him doe his worst.   1725

        ¶Exeunt Shiriffes and Officers.

FAUKENBRIDGE: Ile to Blacke-heath, Ile to the holy Hermit,
[Aside] There shall I knowe not onely these deceivers,
But how my wife playes fast and loose with Richard,
Ha, I shall fit them, Ile tickle them,   1730
Ile doo't, Ile hence, Ile to the Heath amaine.   ¶EXIT.

JOHN: There shall I know, where this damned Gloster is,
Ile have the Devils rous'd to finde that Devill,
Or else Ile conjure the olde Conjurer.
[G]   Ile to Blacke-heath, and there with fiends conspire, 1735
But Ile have Glosters head my hearts desire.   [EXIT.]

RICHARD: Would mad Earle Robyn saw these humouristes.
Twol'd feed him fat with Laughter; O twold fit him,
Where ever he is, I knowe the bare consaite
Is better to him than his daintiest foode,   1740
Well, and it fits mee well, now I have time,
To coort my Lady Faukenbridge at leysure,
Love I emplore thy aide faire Cipria,
Thou sea-borne mother at affections ring,

Shine brightly in thy spheare, that art my starre,   1745
My plannet thou of all lights most beautious,
Be thou to my desires Auspitious.   ¶EXIT.

[Sc. xi. Stepney.]
¶Enter ROBERT Hood in the Lady Faukenbridges gowne,
night attire on his head.

ROBERT: O for this Lady, was never poore Gentleman troubled
with Gentlewoman as I am with my selfe, my Lady Faukenbridge
hath fitted me a turne, heere I am visited with sleevelesse
errands and with asking for this thing Madam and that thing
Madam, that they make me almost mad in earnest. Whoop heer's
another Client.   1756

¶Enter a SERVINGMAN.

SERVINGMAN: Heer's my Lady Rawfords Page attends to speake
with your Ladyship.

ROBERT: I pray ye bid her Ladyships Page come into my 1760
Ladiship:

[EXIT SERVINGMAN.]

Well Robin Hood, part with these pettycoates,
And cast these loose devices from thy backe,
Ile nere goe more untrust, never bee kercheft.   1765
Never have this adoe, with what doe you lacke?

¶Enter PAGE.

PAGE: Madam my Lady greets your honour kindely,
And sends you the first grapes of her young vine.

ROBERT: I am much indebted to her honour, thers an angel 1770
for you to drinke; set them up till after supper, Humphery.
Pray looke about for Blocke, Humphery; trust mee I thinke the
foole be lost.

PAGE: No forsooth, Madam hee's upon the greene Jesting with a
stammerer, one Redcap.   1775

[G^v]   ROBERT: It is a lewd fellowe, pray bid him come in youth, Ile
give him his welcome at the doore: commend me to your Lady, I
pray ye hartily.

¶Exit PAGE.

Humphrey, I marvell where sir Richard is so late?   1780
truely, truely hee does not as beseemes a gentleman of his

calling, pray let some goe foorth to meete him on the greene, and send in that blockehead Blocke.   ¶EXIT HUMPHREY.

¶Enter REDCAP and BLOCKE after him.

BLOCKE: Wil ye tel tales ye asse, will ye?   1785

REDCAP: Ile te te tell your La La Lady or I would to g God we were ha hang'd else, as my fa father should have bin.

ROBERT: Now what's the matter there I pray you? what company have you there a gods name? where spend you the day I pray?

BLOCKE: Why where you gave me leave, at the gallows I was, no farther.   1791

REDCAP: A a and you be his La Lady, you are the La Lady Fau Faukenbridge, the Earle of Glo Glosters sister.

ROBERT: I am so fellow.

REDCAP: Y y your man b b Blocke heere, does no nothing 1795 but f f floute m me, a and cr cries r run Re Redcap and s s see your f f father ha ha hang'd. I sh shal g go neere to m make m murder and he u use it.

ROBERT: Wel sirra, leave your mocking you were best, Ile bob your beetle head and if you mocke him.   1800

BLOCKE: He's run Redcap.

REDCAP: La la law ma Madam.

ROBERT: Away ye saucy foole, goe waite within.

BLOCKE: Run Redcap, run Redcap.   ¶EXIT.

ROBERT: Art thou the Porters sonne, that was condemned about my brother Gloster?   1806

REDCAP: I G G God be with ye, I am the P P Porters son, I mu must r run to s s seeke your b br brother.

ROBERT: Wel, drinke that fellow, if thou finde my brother bee not too violent, and Ile reward thee.   1810

REDCAP: I th th thanke ye h hartily, and I had not bin cousoned with Sk Skinke, I had no nee need of these Ja Jaunts, for Gl Gloster was s safe enough.

[G2]   ¶Enter BLOCKE and the PORTER with his Cloake muffled.

BLOCKE: Ah farewel Redcap.   1815

REDCAP: Fa Fare we wel and be ha hang'd.   ¶EXIT.

ROBERT: You'll never leave your knavery, whose there more?

BLOCKE: One Madam that hath commendations to you from your
brother.   1819

ROBERT: Commest thou from Gloster? thou art welcome friend.

BLOCKE: O it's one of the kindest Ladies (though she wil now
and then have about with Block) that ever breath'd, and she
had been in her mood now, Redcap would have made her such sp
sp sport as 'a pa pa past.

ROBERT: Wil you make sport and see who knockes againe?   1825

BLOCKE: Our gates are like an Anvile, from foure to ten,
nothing but knicke a knocke upon't.   ¶EXIT.

ROBERT: Wil you be gone sir? honest friend I am glad
My brother Gloster got thy liberty,
Whose flight was cause of thy captivity: 1830
Nor shal there be in us such negligence,
Though thou have lost thy Office and thy house,
But we wil see thee better farre provided,
Than when thou wert porter in the Fleete.

                    ¶Enter BLOCKE.   1835

BLOCKE: Madam your olde friend Prince Richard,
    All alone,
    Making mone,
    Fetching many a greevous grone,

ROBERT: Prince Richard come so late? lights to his chamber,
Sirra, in any case say I am sicke.   1841

BLOCKE: Very sicke, sicke and like to dye: Ile sing it and you
wil.

ROBERT: Away ye knave, tel him, in the morning
Ile humbly waite upon his excellence.   1845

BLOCKE: That's all his desire to have ye lowly and humble, and
tis a courteous thing in a Lady.   ¶EXIT.

ROBERT: Hence, or else ile set you hence: goe in good Friend.

                    [Exit PORTER.]

Come Lady Faukenbridge, it's time to come,   1850
Robin can holde out no longer I see,
Hot wooers will be tempters presently.   ¶EXIT.

[Sc. xii. Blackheath.]
¶Enter SKINKE like an Hermit.

SKINKE: Now holy Skinke in thy religious weed,   1855
Looke out for purchase, or thy wonted clyants:
[G2ᵛ] Warrents quoth you, I was fairly warrented,
Young Robin Hood the Earle of Huntington,
Shalt never fetch me more unto his Prince.

¶Enter LADIE Faukenbridge in Merchants wives attyre.

But PAUCA VERBA Skinke, a prize, a prize,   1861
By th'mas a pretty girle, close Hermit close,
Ore-heare if thou canst, what she desires,
For so my cunning and my credit spreads.

LADY: See how affection armes my feeble strength,   1865
To this so desperate journeying all alone,
While Robin Hood young Earle of Huntington,
Playes Lady Faukenbridge for me at home.

SKINKE: What mistery is this? the Lady Faukenbridge,
It's she, sweet fortune thou hast sent her wel,   1870
I will intice this morcell to my Cell:
Her husband's jealious, I will give him cause,
As he beleeves, I hope it shall succeed;
Nay swounds it shal, she's mine in scorne of speed.

LADY: By this broad beaten path, it should appeare,   1875
The holy Hermits Cave cannot be farre,
And if I erre not, this is he himselfe.

SKINKE: What honour'd tongue enquereth for the Hermit?

LADY: What honour'd tongue?

SKINKE: I Lady Faukenbridge,
I know ye, and I know for what you come,   1880
For Gloster and your husbands jealousie.

LADY: O thou, whose eye of contemplation,
Lookes through the windows of the highest heavens,
Resolve thy Hand-maide, where Earle Gloster lives;
And whether he shall live, and scape the hate,   1885
Of proude young Henry and his brother John?

SKINKE: Ile have you first in, Ile tel you more anone.

Madam, they say bushes have eares and eyes,
And these are matters of great secrecy:
And you'll vouchsafe enter my holy Cell,   1890
There what you long to know, ile quickly tell.

              ¶Enter JOHN and FAUKENBRIDGE.

LADY: Stay heere are strangers.

[G3]   SKINKE: [Aside] A plague upon them, come they in the nicke,
To hinder Raynald of his Foxes tricke?   1895

JOHN: Good day olde Hermit.

FAUKENBRIDGE: So to you faire Dame.

JOHN: By Elinors gray eye she's faire indeed;
Sweet heart come ye for holy benizons?
Hermit hast thou good custome with such Cliants?
I cannot blame your feates, your jugling trickes,   1900
Plague juggle you.

LADY: Why cursse ye sacred worth?

FAUKENBRIDGE: Ill done in sooth my Lord, very ill done,
Wrong holinesse: [Aside] a very pretty woman.
Mocke gravity; [Aside] by the masse a cherry lippe,
A it's not wel done, deride a holy Hermit?   1905

JOHN: I have it in my purse shall make amends.

SKINKE: [Aside] His purse and yours shall make me some
                                    [amends,
For hindring me this morning from the Lady;
For scaring me at Taverne yesternight,
For having backe your chaine, Ile fit you both,   1910

JOHN: Hermit, a word.

FAUKENBRIDGE: A word with you faire mistresse.

JOHN: Where lye your devills that tel all your newes?
Would you would trouble them for halfe an houre,
To know what's become of traytor Gloster,
That in my cloathes brake prison in the Fleete?   1915

SKINKE: No, it was Skinke.

JOHN: Come olde foole yee dote.

SKINKE: But heare me.

FAUKENBRIDGE: Heare him Prince.

JOHN: Swounds who heares you?
Ile make your Lady graft ye for this worke:
But to your tale sir.

SKINKE: Knowe thrise honour'd Prince,
That Skinke did cousen Redcap of his cloathes.   1920
Gloster did couzen Skinke, and so escapt.

JOHN: Well done Faukenbridge?

FAUKENBRIDGE: My Lord he tels you true.

JOHN: You finde it on her lippes: but forward sir.

SKINKE: Twas Skinke in Glosters gowne, whome you did visit,
[G3^v]   That playd at bowles and after stole your cloths,   1925
While you went into the Lord Moortons chamber.

JOHN: This savors of some truth,

FAUKENBRIDGE: Tis very like,

JOHN: Well Faukenbridge by heaven Ile tell your wife.   1928

FAUKENBRIDGE: She'l much beleeve you: [To LADY]   you will
                                                            [come?
Tell me of my wife: [To LADY]   this evening faile me not.
My wife quoth you: [To LADY]   Ile send my wife from home,
Do, tell my wife prince John, by my deare mother,   1932
I love her too too well to like another.

LADY: [Aside] It seems so fox, O what a world is this,
There most sinne raynes where least suspition is,   1935

FAUKENBRIDGE: You'l come.

LADY: I will not faile, I warrant you.

JOHN: Hermit is all this true?

SKINKE: If he himselfe
Deliver not so much before ye sleepe,
Roote me from out the borders of this Realme.

JOHN: Well by your leave sir Richard Faukenbridge,   1940
Hence free from feare, you'l melt, you'l melt olde man,

FAUKENBRIDGE: Nay take her to you, she is a shrow I warrant,
Ile to the holy Hermit, and inquire,
About my chaine, your sword, the Pursevant

And other matters that I have to aske.   1945

SKINKE: Your welcome good sir Richard,

[Exit FAUKENBRIDGE and SKINKE.]

JOHN: Nay doe not
Stand on tearmes, I am fire, all life,
Nor never tell me that I have a wife.   1950
I doe not meane to marry, ye think so,
But to be merry, you the manner knowe.
And you will have me, have me, poynt a meeting,
Ile be your true love, you shall be my sweeting,
If you deny to promise, this is plaine   1955
Ile have my will eare you get home againe.

LADY: Most gratious Lord.

JOHN: Tut tell not me of grace,
I like no goodnes but a beautious face.
Be therefore breefe, give me your hand and sweare,
Or Ile away with you into the heath,   1960
Neither shall Faukenbridge nor Hermit helpe,
[G4] And what I doe Ile answer well enough.

LADY: Why, then my Lord.

JOHN: Nay do not stand on then,
But tell me when my Lord shall have you Lady,
Its presently, ile venter for a baby.   1965

LADY: This night at Stepney by my summer house,
There is a taverne which I sometime use,
When we from London come a gossoping,
It is the Hinde.

JOHN: Give me thy pretty hand.
Thou'lt meet me by the Hinde, Ile be thy Roe,   1970

LADY: One word's enough,

JOHN: Suffice then be it so.

LADY: [Aside] Ile fit my olde adulterer and your grace,
Ile send the Princesse thether in my place.

[Enter FAUKENBRIDGE and SKINKE.]

FAUKENBRIDGE: Prince John, Prince John, the Hermit teles me
                                        [wonders.
He sayes it was Skinke that scapt us at the Taverne,   1976
Skinke had my chaine: nay sure that Skinke did all.

SKINKE: I say goe but to yonder corner,
And ere the Sun be halfe an hower higher,
Ther will the theefe attempt a robery,   1980

JOHN: Who Skinke?

FAUKENBRIDGE: Will Skinke?

SKINKE: I Skinke upon my word.

FAUKENBRIDGE: Shal we goe seaze upon him good Prince John?

JOHN: Nay we will have him, that's no question.
And yet not hurte the honest rogue.
He'll helpe us well in quest of changeing Gloster,   1985
Hermit farwell. [To LADY] Lady keepe your houre.

FAUKENBRIDGE: Adeiu olde Hermit: [Aside] soone in th'evening
                                            Lasse,

LADY: [Aside] Ile meet you both, and meet with both of you.
Father what answere doe you give to me?

SKINKE: Lady start downe I must unto my cell,   1990
Where I am curing of a man late hurt,
He drest, I must unto my Orizons,
In halfe an houre al wil be dispatcht,
And then I will attend your Ladyship.   [EXIT.]

[G4^V] LADY: At your best leasure father, O the life   1995
That this thrise reverend Hermit leadeth heere.
How farre remote from mortall vanities,
Baites to the soule, enticements to the eye?
How farre is he unlike my lustfull Lord?
Who being given himselfe to be unchaste,   2000
Thinke all men like himselfe, in their effects,
And injures me, that never had a thought,
To wrong the sacred rytes of spotlesse faith.

          ¶Enter SKINKE with a patch on his face,
              and a Faulconers lure in his hand.

SKINKE: Hermit farewel, ile pay ye or speake with ye   2006
next time I see yee. Sweete mouse the Hermit bids you stay
heere, he'll visit you anon. [Aside] Now John and
Faukenbridge, Ile match yee, and I doe not, say Skinke's a
wretch, a wren, a worme, when I have trickt them, Madam 2010
I will trimme you. Commodity is to be prefer'd before
pleasure. About profit Skink, for crownes for crownes, that
make the kingly thoughts.   ¶EXIT.

LADY: I am assur'd that man's some murderer,
Good Father Hermit speake and comfort me,   2015
Are ye at prayers goode olde man? I pray ye speake,
What's heere a beard? a counterfeited hayre?
The Hermit's portes? garments and his beades?
Jesus defend me I will fly this denne,
It's some theeves cave, no haunt for holy men.   2020
What if the murderer, (as I ges him one)
Set on my husband, tush Prince John and hee
Are able to defend them noble selves,
How eare, I will not tarry, Ile away,   2024
Least unto theft and rape, I proove apray.   ¶EXIT.

                    [Sc. xiii.   The Same.]
                     ¶Enter SKINKE Solus.

SKINKE: Younder they are Ile fit them, heer's my ground:
Wa ha how, wa ha how?

                    ¶Enters FAUKENBRIDGE.   2030

FAUKENBRIDGE: I warrant ye my Lord some man's distrest.

JOHN: Why man tis a Faulconer,

[H] FAUKENBRIDGE: Mary of me
Good fellow, I did think thou hadst bin robd.

SKINKE: Rob'd, sir no, he that comes to rob me shal have 2034
a hard match on't, yet two good fellows had like to bin rob'd
by one tall theefe, had not I stept in: abots on him, I lost
a hauke by him, and yet I car'd not to send another after him,
so I could find the theefe; and here about he is. I know he is
squatted.   2039

FAUKENBRIDGE: Sayst thou me so? we'l finde him by Saint Mary.
An honest fellow, a good common wealths man.

JOHN: There are caves heereabout good fellow, are there not?

SKINKE: Yes sir, tread the ground sir, and you shal heare
their hollownes, this way sir this way.

JOHN: Help Faukenbridge.

FAUKENBRIDGE: O help me good Prince John.   2045

SKINKE: Ile helpe you both, deliver sir deliver,
Swounds linger not: Prince John put up your pursse,
Or ile throw poniards downe upon your pate.

Quickely, when? I am Skink that scapt ye yesternight, and fled
the Fleete in your cloake, carrying mee cleane out of   2050
winde and raine. I broke the bonds and links that fettered
your chaine amity,

This cheate is mine: Farewel: I cannot stay,
Sweet Prince, olde Knight, I thanke ye for this pray.

FAUKENBRIDGE: Gods mary mother, heer's a jest indeed,   2055
We came to take a theefe, a theefe takes us.
Where are ye good my Lord?

JOHN: No matter where,
I thinke I was fore-spoken at ye teate,
This damn'd rogue serv'd me thus? Gloster and he
Upon my life conclude in villany.   2060
He was not wont to plot these stratagems,
Lend me your hand a little, come away,
Let's to the Cell againe, perchaunce the Hermit
Is Skinke, and theefe, and Hermit al in one.

FAUKENBRIDGE: Mary a God then ten to one its so,   2065
Wel thought on Princely John,
He had my chayne, no doubt he had your swoord.

JOHN: If there be now no Hermit at the Cel,
Ile sweare by al the Saints its none but he.   ¶EXEUNT.

[Sc. xiv. The Same.]
¶Enter GLOSTER in the Hermits gowne,
putting on the beard.

[H^V]   GLOSTER: This accident hath hit thy humour Gloster,
From pursevant ile turne a Hermit now.
Sure he that keeps this Cell is a counterfeit,   2075
Else what does he heere with false hayre and beard?
Well how so eare it be, Ile seeme to be
The holy Hermit: for such fame there is,
Of one accounted reverend on this heath.

¶Enter SKINKE.   2080

SKINKE: Ile faine unto my cell, to my faire Lady,
But John and Faukenbridge are at my heeles,
And some od mate is got into my gowne,
And walkes devoutly like mny counterfeite,
I cannot stay to question with you now,   2085
I have another gowne, and all things fit,
These guests once rid, new mate? Ile bum, Ile marke you.

[Exit SKINKE.]

GLOSTER: What's he a gods name? he is quickly gone,
I am for him, were he Robin-good fellow,   2090

[Enter at another door JOHN and FAUKENBRIDGE.]

Whose yonder the Prince John and Faukenbridge?
I thinke they haunt me like my GENII,
One good the other ill, by th'mass they prye
And looke uppon me but suspitiously.   2095

JOHN: This is not Skinke, the Hermit is not Skinke:
He is a learned reverend holy man.

FAUKENBRIDGE: He is he is a very godly man,
I warrant ye, he's at his booke at's prayers,
Wee should have tooke you, by my hollydam   2100
Even for a very theefe.

GLOSTER: Now God forfend
Such noblemen as you should gesse me so,
I never gave such cause for ought I knowe.

JOHN: Yet thou didst tell us Skinke should doe a roberye,
Appoynted us the place, and there we found him,   2105

FAUKENBRIDGE: And he felt us, for he hath rob'd us both.

GLOSTER: He's a lewd fellow, but he shall be taken.

JOHN: I had rather heere of Gloster then of him.

GLOSTER: Gloster did cheate him, of the same golde chaine,
That deceiv'd Sir Richard Faukenbridge,   2110
He got your sword Prince John: 'twas he that savde
The porter, and beguil'd the Pursevant,

[H2]   JOHN: A vengaunce on him.

GLOSTER: Doo not cursse good Prince,
He's bad enough, twere better pray for him.

JOHN: Ile kill thee, and thou bid me pray for him. 2115
Ile fell woods, and ring thee round with fire,
Make thee an offring unto fierce revenge,
If thou have but a thought to pray for him.

GLOSTER: I am bound to pray for all men, chefely christians.

JOHN: Ha ha, for christians, thinkst thou he is one? 2120
For men: hast thou opinion he is a man?
He that changes himselfe to sundry shapes,

Is he a christian? can he be a man?
O, irreligious thoughts,

GLOSTER: Why worthy Prince,
I saw him christened, dept into the font   2125

JOHN: Then nyne times like the northen laplanders,
He backward circled the sacred Font,
And nyne times backward sayd his Orisons,
As often curst the glorious hoast of heaven,
As many times invock'd the fiends of hell,   2130
And so turn'd witch, for Gloster is a witch.

GLOSTER: Have patients Gentle Prince, he shall appeare,
Before your Kingly father speedily.

JOHN: Shall he indeed? sweet comfort kisse thy cheeke,
Peace circle in thy aged honoured head,   2135
When he is taken: Hermit I protest
Ile build thee up a chappell and a shrine:
Ile have thee worshipt, as a man devine,
Assure me he shall come, and Skinke shall come.

FAUKENBRIDGE: I that same Skinke, I prethee send that Skinke,

JOHN: Send both, and both as prisoners crimminate   2141
Shall forfeite their last lives to England's state,
Which way will Faukenbridge?

FAUKENBRIDGE: Over the water,
And so with al speed I may to Stepney

JOHN: I must to Stepney too, and revile, and be blith,   2145
Olde Knight winke at my mirth, 't may make amends,
So thou, and I, and our friends, may be friends.

FAUKENBRIDGE: Withall my heart, withall my heart Prince John,
Olde Faukenbridge will waite uppon your grace,
[H2ᵛ] Be good to Gloster for my Marrians sake,   2150
And me and myne you shall your servants make,

JOHN: Of that anon my pleasure being serv'd,
Gloster shall have what Gloster hath deserv'd.

FAUKENBRIDGE: Why, that's well said, adew good honest Hermit.

                    ¶Exit.   2155

JOHN: Hermit farwell, if I had my desire,
Ile make the world thy wonderous deeds admire.   ¶EXIT.

GLOSTER: Still good, still passing good, Gloster is still

Henryes true hate, foe to Johns froward will.
No more of that for them in better tyme,   2160
If this same Hermit be an honest man,
He will protect me by this simple life,
If not I care not, Ile be ever Gloster,
Make him my foot stole if he be a slave,
For Basenesse over worth can have no power.   2165
Robin bethinke thee, thou art come from Kings,
Then scorne to be slave to underlings,
Looke well about thee Lad and thou shalt see,
Them burst in envy that would injure thee.
Hermit Ile meet you in your Hermits gowne,   2170
Honest, Ile love you: worse, Ile knocke you downe.   ¶EXIT.

                        [Sc. xv. Stepney.]
              ¶Enter Prince RICHARD with Musicke.

RICHARD: Kinde friends, wee have troubled Lady Faukenbridge,
And eyther she's not willing to be seene,   2175
Or els not well: or with our boldnesse greev'd,
To ease these I have brought you to this window,
Knowing you are in musicke excellent,
I have pend a ditty heere: and I desire
You would sing it for her love and my content.   2180

MUSICIAN: With all my heart my Lord.

                ¶Enter ROBERT Hood like the Lady.

ROBERT: Your excellence forgets your Princely worth,
If I may humbly crave it at your hands,
Let me desire this musicke be dismist.   2185

RICHARD: Forbeare I pray and withdraw your selves.

                      ¶Exeunt MUSICKE.

         Be not offended gratious Marrian,
         Under the upper heaven, nine goodly spheres,
[H3]   Turne with a motion ever musicall,   2190
         In Pallaces of Kings, melodious sounds,
         Offer pleasures to ther soveraignes eares.
         In Temples, milke white clothed queristors,
         Sing sacred Anthemes bowing to the shrine,
         And in the feelds whole quires of winged clarkes, 2195
         Salutes the morning bright and Christaline.
         Then blame not me, you are my heaven, my Queene,
         My saint, my comfort, brighter then the morne,
         To you all musicke, and all praise is due.
         For your delight for you delight was borne,   2200
         The world wold have no mirth, no joy, no day,

If from the world your beautie were away.

ROBERT: Fie on loves blasphemie and forgery,
To call that joy, thats onely misery,
I that am wedded to suspitious age,   2205
Solicited by your lascivious youth,
I that have one poore comforte living,
Gloster my brother, my hie harted brother,
He flies for feare, least he should faint and fall
Into the hands of hate tirannical.   2210

RICHARD: What would you I should doe?

ROBERT: I would full faine,
My brother Gloster had his peace againe.

RICHARD: Shall love be my reward if I doe bring
A certaine token of his good estate,
And after pacifie my brothers wrath?   2215
Say you'l love, we'l be fortunate,

ROBERT: I will.

RICHARD: No more, I vow to dye unblest
If I perform not this imposed quest,
But one word Madam pray can you tell,
Where Huntington my ward is?

ROBERT: I was bold   2220
To send young Robin Hood your noble ward
Upon some busines of import for me.

RICHARD: I am glad he is imployde in your affayres,
Farewell kinde faire, let not one cloudy frowne
Shaddow the bright sunne of thy beauties light.   2225
[H3ᵛ] Be confident in this, ile finde thy brother,
Rayse power but we'l have peace, onely performe
Your gratious promise at my backe returne.

ROBERT: Wel, heer's my hand, Prince Richard that same night
Which secondeth the day of your returne,   2230
Ile be thy bedfellow, and from that houre
Forsweare the loathed bed of Faukenbridge:
Be speedy therefore, as you hope to speed.

RICHARD: O that I were as large wing'd as the winde,
Then should you see my expeditious will: 2235
My most desire, adew, guesse by my haste,
Of your sweet promise the delicious taste.   ¶EXIT.

ROBERT: Why so: I am rid of him by this devise,
He would else have tyred me with his sighes and songs,

¶Enter BLOCKE.   2240

But now I shall have ease, heere comes the Saint,
To whom such sute was made.

BLOCKE: My Lady Gentlewoman is even heere in her privitye
walke, Madam heer's the Marchants wife was heere yesterday
would speake with yee; O I was somewhat bolde to bring 2245
her in.

ROBERT: Wel leave us sir; y'are welcome gentlewoman.

BLOCKE: These women have no liberality in the world in them, I
never let in man to my Lady, but I am rewarded.

ROBERT: Please ye to walke sir? wherefore mumble ye?   2250

LADY: Robin what newes? how hast thou done this night?

ROBERT: My Ladiship hath done my part, my taske,
Lyne all alone for lacke of company,
I might have had Prince Richard.

LADY: Was he heere?

ROBERT: He went away but now;   2255
I have bin lov'd and woo'd too simply,
God rid me of the woman once againe,
Ile not be tempted so for all the world,
Come, wil you to your chamber and uncase?

LADY: Nay keep my habit yet a little while,   2260
Olde Faukenbridge is almost at the gate,
I met him at Black heath just at the Hermits,
And taking me to be a Merchants wife,
[H4] Fell mightily in love, gave me his ring,
Made me protest that I would meete him heere.   2265
I tolde him of his Lady, O tut quoth he,
Ile shake her up, ile packe her out of sight,
He comes kinde Robin Hood, holde up the jest.

¶Enter Sir Richard FAUKENBRIDGE and BLOCKE.

FAUKENBRIDGE: Gods mary knave, how long hath she bin heere?

BLOCKE: Sir she came but even in afore you.   2271

FAUKENBRIDGE: A cunning queane, a very cunning queane,
Go to your busines Block, ile meete with her.

BLOCKE: Ah old Muttonmounger I beleeve heer's worke towards.

¶Exit [BLOCKE.]   2275

FAUKENBRIDGE: Doe not beleeve her Mall, doe not beleeve her:
I onely spake a word or two in jest,
But would not for the world have bin so mad,
Doe not beleeve her Mall, doe not beleeve her:

ROBERT: What should I not beleeve? what doe you meane?   2280

LADY: Why good Sir Richard, let me speake with you.
Alas wil you undoe me? wil you shame me?
Is this your promise? came I heere for this?
To be a laughing stocke unto your Lady?

ROBERT: How now Sir Richard? what's the matter there?   2285

FAUKENBRIDGE: Ile talke with you anon, come hyther woman?
Didst not tel my wife what match we made?

LADY: I tel your wife? thinke ye I am such a beast?
Now God forgive ye, I am quite undone.   2289

FAUKENBRIDGE: Peace duck, peace ducke, I warrant al is wel.

ROBERT: What's the matter? I pray ye sir Richard tell me?

FAUKENBRIDGE: Mary Mall thus, about some twelve monthes
                                          [since,
Your brother Gloster, that mad prodigall,
Caus'd me to passe my word unto her husband,
For some two thousand pound: or more perchaunce,   2295
No matter what it is, you shall not know,
Nay ye shal never aske to know.

ROBERT: And what of this?

FAUKENBRIDGE: Mary the man's decayde,
And I beleeve a little thing would please her;
A very little thing, a thing of nothing.   2300
Goe in good Mall, and leave us two alone,
[H4ᵛ]   [To LADY] Ile deale with ye as simply as I can.

LADY: [Aside] Fox looke about ye, ye are caught yfaith.

ROBERT: Deale with her simply, o ho; what kinde of dealing?
Can ye not deale with her and I be by?   2305

FAUKENBRIDGE: Mary a God, what are ye jealous?
Ye teach me what to doe: in, get you in.
O I have heard Prince Richard was your guest,
How dealt you than? In, get you in I say,
Must I take care about your brothers debts,   2310

And you stand crossing me, in, or ile send you in.

¶Exit ROBIN.

Ha sirra, you'l be master, you'l weare the yellow,
You'l be an over-seer: mary shal yee.

LADY: Ye are too curst (me thinkes sir) to your Lady;   2315

FAUKENBRIDGE: Ah wench content thee, I must beare her hard,
Else she'l be prying into my dalliances:
I am an olde man sweeet girle I must be merry,
All steele, al spright, keep in health by change,
Men may be wanton, women must not range.   2320

LADY: You have given good counsel sir, ile repent me,
Heer's your ring, ile onely love my husband.

FAUKENBRIDGE: I meane not so, I thinke to day thou toldes me
Thy husband was an unthrift, and a bankrout,
And he be so, tut thou hast favour store,   2325
Let the knave beg, beauty cannot be poore.

LADY: Indeed my husband is a bankrout,
Of faith, of love, of shame, of chastity,
Dotes upon other women more then me.

FAUKENBRIDGE: Ha doe he so? then give him tit for tat,   2330
Have one so young and faire, and loves another,
He's worthy to be coockolded by the masse.
What is he olde or young?

LADY: About your age.

FAUKENBRIDGE: An olde knave and cannot be content with
                                [such a peate,
Come to my closet girle, make much of me,   2335
We'll appoint a meeting place some twice a weake,
And ile maintaine thee like a Lady, ha?

LADY: O but you'll forget me presently,
When you looke well upon your Ladies beauty.

[I]   FAUKENBRIDGE: Who upon her? why she is a very dowdy,   2340
A dishclout, a foule Jipsie unto thee,
Come to my closet lasse, there take thy earnest
Of love, of pleasure and good maintenaunce.

LADY: I am very fearefull.

FAUKENBRIDGE: Come foole never feare
I am Lord heare, who shall disturb us then?
                                            2345

Nay come, or by the rood Ile make you come,

LADY: Help Madam Faukenbridge for gods sake.

¶Enter ROBERT Hood and BLOCKE.

FAUKENBRIDGE: How now, what meanst?

LADY: Help Gentle Madam help,

ROBERT: How now what aylst thou?   2350

BLOCKE: Nay and't be a woman, neare feare my master Madam,

ROBERT: Why speakst thou not, what aylst thou?

FAUKENBRIDGE: Why nothing, by the rood nothing she ayls.

LADY: O Madam this vile man would have abused me,
And forct me to his closset,

ROBERT: [Aside] Ah olde cole,   2355
Now looke about, you are catcht.
Call in your fellowes Blocke,

FAUKENBRIDGE: Doe not thou knave,

ROBERT: Doe or Ile crack your crowne,

BLOCKE: Nay Ile doo't, I know she meanes to shame you.
                                        [¶EXIT.

FAUKENBRIDGE: Why Mall wilt thou beleeve this paultrie woman?
Huswife Ile have you whipt for slaundring me.   2361

ROBERT: What Leacher, no she is an honest woman,
Her husband's well knowne, all the houshold knowes.

BLOCKE: Heer's some now, to tell all the towne your mynd.

ROBERT: Before ye all I must sure complaine,   2365
You see this wicked man, and ye all knowe
How oft he hath byn Jealous of my life,
Suspecting falshood being false himselfe;

BLOCKE: O maister, O maister,

FAUKENBRIDGE: She slaunders me. She is a cousoning queane,
Fetch me the Constable, Ile have her punisht,   2371

LADY: The Constable for me fie, fie upon ye.
Madam do you know this ring?

ROBERT: It is sir Richards.

[I^V] BLOCKE: O I, that's my maisters too sure.

FAUKENBRIDGE: I mary, I did lend it to the false drab   2375
To fetch some money for that bankrout knave
Her husband, that lyes prisoner in the Fleete.

LADY: My husband bankrout? my husband in the Fleete prisoner?
No, no, he is as good a man as you.

ROBERT: I that he is, and can spend pound for pound   2380
With thee yfaith, wert richer then thou art,
I know the gentleman.

LADY: Nay Madam he is hard by,
There must be Revelles at the Hinde to night;
Your copesmate there, Prince John.

ROBERT: Ther's a hot youth.   2385

BLOCKE: O a fierce Gentleman.

LADY: He was fierce as you, but I have matcht him,
The Princesse shall be there in my attyre.

FAUKENBRIDGE: A plaguy crafty queane, mary a God
I see Prince John coorted as well as I,   2390
And since he shall be mockt as well as I,
Its some contentment.

BLOCKE: Masse he droopes, fellow Humphrey, he is almost taken,
looke about ye old Richard?

FAUKENBRIDGE: Hence knaves, get in a little, prethee Mall
Let thou and I and she, shut up this matter.   2396

ROBERT: Away sirs, get in.

BLOCKE: Come, come let's goe, he will be baited now, farewel
old Richard.   ¶EXIT.

ROBERT: Now sir, what say you now?

FAUKENBRIDGE: Mary sweet Mall,   2400
I say I met this woman, likt her, lov'd her,
For she is worthy love I promise thee;
I say I coorted her: tut make no braule
Twixt thou and I, we'l have amends for all.

ROBERT: Had I done such a tricke, what then? what then? 2405

FAUKENBRIDGE: Ah prethee Mall, tut beare with men.

ROBERT: I, we must beare with you; you'l be excus'd,
When women undeserved are abus'd.

FAUKENBRIDGE: Nay doe not weep, pardon me gentle Lady,
I know thee vertuous, and I doo protest,   2410
Never to have an evill thought of thee.

[I2] ROBERT: I, ye sweare, who's that that will beleeve ye?

FAUKENBRIDGE: Now by my holydam and honest faith,
This Gentlewoman shall witnes what I sweare.
Sweet Ducke a little help me?

LADY: Trust him Madam.   2415

FAUKENBRIDGE: I will be kinde, credulous, constant ever,
Doe what thou wilt, ile be suspitious never.

ROBERT: For which I thanke noble Faukenbridge.

[Removes his disguise.]

FAUKENBRIDGE: Body of me who's this? yong Huntington?   2420

[LADY removes her disguise.]

LADY: And I your Lady whome you coorted last,
Ye lookt about you ill, foxe we have caught ye,
I met ye at Blacke heath, and ye were hot.

FAUKENBRIDGE: I knew thee Mall, now by my swoord I knew thee,
I winkt at all, I laught at every jest.   2426

ROBERT: I he did winke, the blinde man had an eye.

FAUKENBRIDGE: Peace Robin, thou't once be a man as I.

LADY: Well, I must beare it all.

FAUKENBRIDGE: Come, and ye beare,
Its but your office, come forget sweet Mall.   2430

LADY: I doe forgive it, and forget it sir.

FAUKENBRIDGE: Why that's well said, that's done like
                              [a good girle:
Ha sirra, ha you matcht me pretty Earle?

ROBERT: I have, ye see sir, I must unto Blacke heath,

In quest of Richard, whom I sent to seeke   2435
Earle Gloster out, I know he's at the Hermits;
Lend me your Coach; Ile shift me as I ride,
Farewell sir Richard.   ¶EXIT.

FAUKENBRIDGE: Farewell Englands pride,
By the mattins Mall it is a pretty childe;
Shall we goe meete John? shall we goe mocke the Prince? 2440

LADY: We will.

FAUKENBRIDGE: O then we shall have sport anon,
Never weare yellow Mall, twas but a tricke,
Olde Faukenbridge wil stil be a mad Dicke.   ¶EXEUNT.

              [Sc. xvi. Blackheath.]
             ¶Enter REDCAP and GLOSTER.

REDCAP: Doe ye s s say fa fa father Hermit, th that Gl Gloster
is about this Heath?   2447

GLOSTER: He is upon this Heath, Sonne looke about it,
Run but the compasse, thou shalt finde him out,

[12ᵛ] REDCAP: R r run? ile r run the co compasse of all K Kent 2450
but Ile f finde him out, my f f father (where ere hee layes
his head) dare ne never co come home I know, t t till hee bee
fo fo found.

GLOSTER: Wel thou shalt find him, knowst thou who's a
                                        [hunting?

REDCAP: M m mary tis the Earles of La La Lancaster and 2460
Le Leyster. Fa fa farewell f father, and I finde Skink or Glo
Gloster, Ile g g give thee the pr prise of a penny p p pudding
for thy p paines.   ¶EXIT.

GLOSTER: Adew good friend: this is sure the fellow
I sent on message from the Parlament.   2465
The Porters sonne, he's still in quest of me,
And Skinke that cousoned him of his red cap.

             ¶Enter RICHARD like a Serving man.

But looke about thee Gloster, who comes yonder?
O a plaine servingman, and yet perhaps   2470
His bags are lyn'd, and my pursse now growes thin:
If he have any I must share with him.

             ¶Enter SKINKE like a Hermit.

And who's on yond side? O it is my Hermit,
Hath got his other sute since I went foorth.   2475

SKINKE: Sbloud yonder's company, ile backe againe,
Else I would be with you counterfeite,
Ile leave the rogue till opportunity,
But never eate till I have quit my wrong.   ¶EXIT.

RICHARD: I saw two men attend like holy Hermits,   2480
One's slipt away, the other's at his beades,
Now Richard for the love of Marian,
Make thy inquiry where mad Gloster lives.
If England or the verge of Scotland holde him,
Ile seeke him thus disguis'd: if he be past   2485
To any forraigne part; ile follow him.
Love thou art Lord of hearts, thy lawes are sweet,
In every troubled way, thou guidst our feete.
Lovers injoin'd to passe the daungerous Sea
Of big swolne sorrow, in the Barke affection;   2490
The windes and waves of woe need never feare,
While Love, the helme doth like a Pylate steare.

GLOSTER: Heer's some lover come, a mischiefe on him,
[I3]   I know not how to answere these mad fooles,
But ile be briefe, ile marre the Hermits tale;   2495
Off gowne, holde Buckler, slice it bilbowe blade.

RICHARD: What's this? what should this meane? old man,
                                    [good friend

GLOSTER: Young foole deliver else see your end.

RICHARD: I thought thou hadst been holy and a Hermit.

GLOSTER: What ere you thought, your pursse? come quickly sir?
Cast that upon the ground, and then conferre.   2501

RICHARD: There it is.

GLOSTER: Falles it so heavy? then my heart is light.

RICHARD: Thou't have a heavy heart before thou touch it,
Theft shrinde in holy weedes? stand to't y'are best.   2505

GLOSTER: And if I doe not, seeing such a pray,
Let this be to me a disaster day.

                    ¶Fight and part once or twise.

RICHARD: Art thou content to breath?

GLOSTER: With all my heart,

Take halfe thy money and we'l friendly part.   2510

RICHARD: I will not cherish theft.

GLOSTER: Then I defy thee.

                    ¶Fight againe and breath.

RICHARD: [Aside] Alas for pitty, that so stout a man,
So reverend in aspect, should take this course.

GLOSTER: [Aside] This is no common man with whom I fight,
And if he be, he is of wondrous spright,   2516
Shall we part stakes?

RICHARD: Fellow take the pursse
Upon condition thou wilt follow me?

GLOSTER: What waite on you? weare a turn'd Livery?
Whose man's your master? If I be your man,   2520
My man's office will be excellent:
There lyes your pursse againe, win it and weare it.   ¶FIGHT.

           ¶Enter ROBERT Hood, they breath, offer againe.

ROBERT: Clashing of weapons at my welcome hyther?
Bickring upon Blacke-heath, well said olde man,   2525
Ile take thy side, the yonger hath the oddes.
Stay, end your quarrell, or I promise ye
Ile take the olde mans part.

RICHARD: You were not wont
Yong Huntington, be stil on Richards side.

ROBERT: Pardon gratious Prince I knew ye not.   2530

GLOSTER: Prince Richard: then lye envy at his foote,
Pardon thy cousen Gloster, valiant Lord,
[13ᵛ] I knew no common force confronted myne,

RICHARD: O heaven I had the like conseite of thine.
I tell thee Robin Gloster thou art met,   2535
Bringing such comfort unto Richards heart,
As in the foyle of warre when dust and sweat,
The thirst of wreake, and the Sunnes fiery heate,
Have seazd uppon the soule of valiaunce,
And he must faint except he be refresht.   2540
To me thou comst as if to him should come,
A perry from the North, whose frostie breath
Might fan him coolnesse in that doubt of death.
With me thou meets, as he a spring might meet,
Cooling the earth under his toyle partcht feet,   2545

Whose cristall moysture in his Helmit taine,
Comforts his spyrits, makes him strong againe.

GLOSTER: Prince, in short termes if you have brought me
                                              [comfort
Know if I had my pardon in this hand
That smit base Skinke in open Parlament,   2550
I would not come to Court, till the high feast
Of your proud brothers birth day be expyred,
For as the olde King as he made a vow
At his unluckie Coronation,
Must waite upon the boy and fill his cuppe,   2555
And all the Pieres must kneele while Henrie kneeles
Unto his cradle; he shall hang me up,
Eare I commit that vile Idolatrie.
But when the feast is past if you'll befrend me,
Ile come and brave my proude foes to their teeth.   2560

RICHARD: Come Robin, and if my brothers grace denye,
Ile take thy parte, them and their threates defye.

GLOSTER: Gramercy Princely Dicke,

ROBERT: I have some power,
I can rayse two thousand Soldiers in an hower,

GLOSTER: Gramercy Robin, gramercy little wag,   2565
Prince Richard, pray let Huntington
Carry my sister Faukenbridge this ring,

RICHARD: Ile carry it my selfe, but I had rather
Had thy kinde company, thou mightst have mov'd
[I4]   Thy Sister, whome I long have vainely lov'd,   2670

GLOSTER: I like her that she shunnes temptation
Prince Richard, but I beare with doting lovers,
I should not take it well, that you urge me
To such an office: but I beare with you,
Love's blind and mad, hie to her boldly, try her;   2575
But if I know she yeeld, faith Ile defie her.

RICHARD: I like thy honorable resolution,
Gloster I pray thee pardon my intreate.

GLOSTER: Its mens custome; part part Gentle Prince,
Farwell good Robin this gold I will borrow,   2580
Meet you at Stepney pay you all tomorrow.

ROBERT: Adew Gloster,

GLOSTER: Farwell, be short;
You gone, I hope to have a little sport.

RICHARD: Take heed mad Cuz.   ¶EXEUNT.

GLOSTER: Tut tell not me of heed,
He that's too wary never hath good speed.   2585

                    ¶Hollowing within,
        Enter LANCASTER with a broken staffe in his hand.

Whose this old Lancaster my honored frend?

LANCASTER: These knaves have serv'd me well, left me alone,
I have hunted fairely, lost my purse, my chaine,   2590
My Jewels, and bin bangd by a bold knave.
Clad in a Hermits gowne like an olde man,
O what a world is this?

GLOSTER: Its ill my Lord.

LANCASTER: Hee's come againe, O knave tis the worse for thee,
Keepe from me, be content with that thou hast,   2595
And see thou flie this heath, for if I take thee,
Ile make thee to all theeves a spectacle,
Had my staffe held, thou hadst not scaped me so,
But come not neare me, follow not thou art best,
Holla, Earle Leyster, holla Huntsman hoe?   [EXIT.]

GLOSTER: Uppon my life, old Lancaster a Hunting,   2601
Hath met my fellow Hermit, could I meet him,
Ide play rob theefe, at least part stakes with him.

                    [Enter SKINKE.]

SKINKE: Zounds he is yonder alone,   2605

                ¶Enter REDCAP with a cudgell.

        Skinke now revenge thy selfe on yonder slave,
        Znayles still prevented? this same Redcap rogue
[14ᵛ]   Runs like hob-goblin up and downe the heath.

REDCAP: Wh wh whope He Hermit, ye ha ha' ma ma made Re Redcap
run a fine co co compasse, ha have you not?   2611

SKINKE: I made thee run?

GLOSTER: Younders my evill Angell,
Were redcap gone, Gloster would conjure him.

REDCAP: Je Je Jesus bl blesse me, whop to to two Hermits? Ile
ca ca caperclaw to to t'one of yee, for momo mocking me, 2615
and I d d doo not ha ha hang me: wh wh   which   is   the   fa   fa

false k k k knave? for I am s s sure the olde He He Hermit wo
would never mo mocke an honest man.

GLOSTER: He is the counterfet he mockt thee fellow.
I did not see thee in my life before,   2620
He weares my garments, and has coussoned me,

REDCAP: Have you co co cousoned   the   he   Hermit   and   m   made
Redcap run to no pu pu purpose?

SKINKE: No he's counterfet I will tell no lyes,
As sure as Skinke deceiv'd thee of thy clothes,   2625
Sent thee to Kent, gave thee thy fare by water,
So sure hee's false, and I the perfet Hermit.

GLOSTER: [Aside] This villaine is a conjurer I doubt,
Were he the devill yet I would not budge.

REDCAP: Si si sirra, you are the co counterfeite, O this 2630
is the tr tr true He Hermit, sta sta stand still g good man at
that, ile bu bumbast you yfaith, ile make you g give the   olde
m m man his gowne.

        ¶Offers to strike, GLOSTER trippes up his heeles,
              shifts SKINKE into his place.

G g gods lid are ye gogood at that? ile cu cudgell yee f 2636
f for this tr tr tricke.

SKINKE: It was not I twas he that cast thee downe,

REDCAP: You li li li lye you ra ra rascall you, I le left ye
st standing he heare.   2640

SKINKE: Zounds hold you stammerer, or Ile cut your stumps.

GLOSTER: He's for me, he's weapon'd, I like that.

REDCAP: O heer's a ro ro rogue in ca ca carnat, help, mu
murder murder.   2644

        ¶Enter LANCASTER and Huntsmen at one doore, LEYSTER
                  and Huntsmen at another.

[K]   LANCASTER: Lay holde upon that theevish counterfeit,

LEYSTER: Why heares another Hermit Lancaster:

GLOSTER: I am the Hermit sir, that wretched man
Doth many a robberie in my disguise: 2650

SKINKE: Its he that robs, he slaunders me, he lies.

LANCASTER: Which set on thee?

REDCAP: Th this f f fellow has a s s sword and a buckler.

LANCASTER: Search him; this is the theefe, o heares my purse,
My chaine, my Jewels: oh thou wicked wretch,   2655
How darst thou under show of holines,
Commit such actions of impietie?
Bind him, Ile have him made a publicke scorne.

SKINKE: Lay holde upon that other hermit,
He is a counterfeit as well as I,   2660
He stole those clothes from me, for I am Skinke,
Search him, I know him not, he is some slave.

GLOSTER: Thou lyest base varlet.

REDCAP: O g God he has a sword too, S Skinke are you ca
catcht?   2665

LANCASTER: Villaine thou shalt with me unto the Court.

LEYSTER: And this with me, this is the traytor Gloster.

GLOSTER: Thou lyest proud Leyster, I am no traytor.

REDCAP: G gloster? O b brave, now m my father sh shall be f
free.   2670

LANCASTER: Earle Gloster I am sorry thou art taken.

GLOSTER: I am not taken yet, nor will I yeild
To any heare but noble Lancaster,
Let Skinke be Leysters prisoner Ile be thine.

LEYSTER: Thou shalt be mine.

GLOSTER: First through a crimson sluce,
Ile send thy hated soule to those blacke fiendes   2676
That long have hovered gaping for their parte,
When tyrant life should leave thy traytor heart.
Come Lancaster keep Skinke ile goe with thee,
Let loose the mad knave, for I prayse his shifts,   2680
He shall not starte away, ile be his guide,
And with proude looks outface young Henries pride.

LEYSTER: Looke to them Lancaster upon thy life.

REDCAP: Well ile r r run and get a p pardon of the K K K King,
Gl Gloster and Skinke ta ta taken? O b b brave, r r r 2685
[K^v] run re/Re Redca cap a and ca ca cary the first n n newes to co

co court.

LEYSTER: Lancaster ile helpe to guarde them to the Court.

LANCASTER: Doe as you please.

GLOSTER: Leyster doe not come neare me,
For if thou doe, thou shalt buy it dearely.   2690

LEYSTER: Ile have thy hand for this.

GLOSTER: Not for thy heart.

SKINKE: Brave Earle, had Skinke knowne thou hadst been the
Noble Gloster (whose mad tricks have made mee love thee) I
would have dy'd Blacke heath red with the bloud of millions,
ere we would have been taken; but what remedy, we are 2695
fast and must answere it like Gentlemen, like Souldiers, like
resolutes.

GLOSTER: I ye are a gallant, come olde Lancaster,
For thy sake will I goe; or else by heaven
Ide send some dozen of these slaves to hel.   ¶EXEUNT. 2700

                    [Sc. xvii. Stepney.]
      ¶Enter Prince RICHARD, ROBERT Hoode and LADY Faukenbridge.

LADY: Your travaile and your comfortable newes,
This Ring, the certaine signe you met with him,
Bindes me in duetyous love unto your grace: 2705
But on my knees I fall, and humbly crave,
Importune that no more, you nere can have.

RICHARD: Nay then ye wrong me Lady Faukenbridge,
Did you not joine your faire white hand with myne?
Swore that ye would forsweare your husbands bed,   2710
If I could but finde out Gloster?

LADY: I sweare so?

RICHARD: By heaven

ROBERT: Take heed, its a high oath my Lord.

RICHARD: What meanst thou Huntington?

ROBERT: To save your soule,
I doe not love to have my friends forsworne.
She never promist that you urge her with.   2715

RICHARD: Goe to, provoke me not.

ROBERT: I tell you true,
Twas I in her attyre that promist you,
She was gone unto the wizard at Blacke heath,
And there had suters more then a good many.

RICHARD: Was I deluded then?

[K2]   LADY: No not deluded,   2720
But hindred from desire unchast and rude:
O let me wooe yee with the tongue of ruth,
Dewing your Princely hand with pitties teares,
That you would leave this most unlawful sute,
If ere we live till Faukenbridge be dead,   2725
(As God defend his death I should desire)
Then if your highnes daine so base a match,
And holy lawes admit a mariage,
Considering our affinity in bloud,
I will become your Handmayde not your harlot,   2730
That shame shall never dwell upon my brow.

ROBERT: Ifaith my Lord she's honorably resolv'd,
For shame no more, importune her no more.

RICHARD: Marian I see thy vertue, and commend it,
I know my error seeking thy dishonor,   2735
But the respectlesse, reasonles commaund
Of my inflamed love, bids me still try,
And trample under foote all pietye.
Yet for I will not seeme too impyous,
Too inconsiderate of thy seeming griefe,   2740
Vouchsafe to be my Mistris: use me kindely,
And I protest Ile strive with all my power,
That lust himselfe may in his heate devour.

LADY: You are my servant then.

RICHARD: Thanks sacred Mistresse.

ROBERT: What am I?

LADY: You are my fellow Robert.   2745

        ¶Enter FAUKENBRIDGE in his hose and dublet.

FAUKENBRIDGE: What Prince Richard? noble Huntington?
Welcome, yfaith welcome, by the morrow Masse
You are come as fitly as my heart can wish:
Prince John this night will be a Reveller,   2750
He hath invited me and Marian.
Gods mary mother goe along with us,
Its but hard by, close by, at our towne Taverne.

RICHARD: Your Taverne?

FAUKENBRIDGE: O I I I tis his owne made match,
Ile make you laugh, ile make you laugh yfaith;   2755
[K2ᵛ] Come, come, he's ready, O come, come away.

LADY: But wher's the Princesse?

FAUKENBRIDGE: She's ready too,
Block Block my man, must be her waiting man,
Nay wil ye goe? for gods sake let us goe.

RICHARD: Is the jest so? nay then let us away.   2760

ROBERT: O twill allay his heate, make dead his fire.

FAUKENBRIDGE: Ye bob'd me first, ye first gave me my hyre,
But come agods name, Prince John stayes for us.   ¶EXEUNT.

ROBERT: This is the world, ever at spend-thriftes feastes,
They are guld themslves, and scoft at by their guests. ¶EXIT.

                    [Sc. xviii. The Hind Tavern.]
                         ¶Enter JOHN.

JOHN: Baffild and scoft,   2768
Skinke, Gloster, women, fooles and boyes abuse me?
Ile be reveng'd.

RICHARD: Reveng'd, and why good childe?
Olde Faukenbridge hath had a worser basting.

FAUKENBRIDGE: I, they have banded me from chase to chase;
I have been their tennis ball, since I did coort,

RICHARD: Come John, take hand with vertuous Isabell,
And let's unto the Court like loving friends,   2775
Our Kingly brothers birth daies feastivall,
Is foorth with to be kept, thether we'l hye,
And grace with pompe that great solemnity.

JOHN: Whether ye will, I care not where I goe:
If griefe wil grace it, ile adorne the shew.   2780

FAUKENBRIDGE: Come Madam, we must thither, we are bound.

LADY: I am loath to see the Court, Gloster being from thence,
Or kneele to him that gave us this offence.

FAUKENBRIDGE: Body of me peace woman, I prethee peace.

¶Enter REDCAP.   2785

REDCAP: Go go god ye, go god s speed ye,

JOHN: Whether run you sir knave?

REDCAP: R r run ye sir knave? why I r run to my La La Fa
Faukenbridge, to te te tell her Sk Skinke and Gl Gkloster is t
taken, and are g g gone to the C C Court with L Lord Leyster,
and L Lord La La Lancaster.   2791

JOHN: Is Gloster taken? thether will I flye
Upon wraths wings, not quiet til he dye.

¶Exit with PRINCESSE.

[K3] RICHARD: Is Gloster taken?   2795

REDCAP: I he is ta taken I wa warrant ye with a wi witnes,

RICHARD: Then will I to Court,
And eyther set him free, or dye the death,
Follow me Faukenbridge, feare not faire Madam:
You said you had the Porter in your House,   2800
Some of your servants bring him, on my life
One hayre shall not be taken from his head,
Nor he, nor you, nor Gloster injured.

FAUKENBRIDGE: Come Mall, and Richard say the word nere feare.

ROBERT: Madam, we have twenty thousand at our call,   2805
The most, young Henry dares, is but to braule.

LADY: Pray God it proove so.

RICHARD: Follow Huntington:
Sir Richard doe not faile to send the Porter.

FAUKENBRIDGE: Blocke, bring the Porter of the Fleete to
[Court.

BLOCKE: I wil sir.   2810

REDCAP: The P P Porter of the Fl Fl Fleete to Court? what P P
Porter of the Fl Fl Fleete?

BLOCKE: What Redcap, run redcap, wilt thou see thy father?

REDCAP: My fa father? I that I wo wold s see my f father, and
there be a p p Porter in your ho house, its my f father. 2815

BLOCKE: Follow me Redcap then.   ¶EXIT.

BLOCKE: Follow me Redcap then.   ¶EXIT.

REDCAP: And you were tw tw twenty B Blockes, ide f f follow ye
s so I would, and r run to the co co court too, and k kn
kneele before the K K King f f for his pardon.

BLOCKE WITHIN: Come away Redcap, run Redcap.   2820

REDCAP: I I I r r run as f f fast as I I ca ca can run I wa
warrant yee.   ¶EXIT.

                    [Sc. xix. Westminster.]
        ¶Enter a Sinet, first two Herraldes, after them LEYSTER
with a Scepter, LANCASTER with a Crowne Imperiall on a   2825
cushion: After them [KING] Henry the elder bareheaded, bearing
a swoord and a Globe: after him young HENRY Crowned: Elinor
the mother QUEENE Crowned: YOUNG QUEENE Crowned. Henry the
elder places his Sonne, the two Queenes on eyther hand,
himselfe at his feete, LEYSTER and LANCASTER below him.   2830

HENRY: Herrald, fetch Lancaster and Leyster Coronets,
       Suffer no Marquesse, Earle, nor Countesse enter,
[K3ᵛ] Except their temples circled are in golde,

        ¶He delivers Coronets to LEYSTER and LANCASTER.

Shew them our vize-roys: by our will controld   2835
As at a coronation, every Peere
Appeares in all his pompe, so at this feast
Held for our birth-right, let them be adorn'd.
Let Gloster be brought in, crowned like an Earle,   ¶EXIT.
This day we'll have no parley of his death,   2840
But talke of Jouisanes and gleeful mirth.
Let Skinke come in, give him a Barons seat,
High is his spirrit, his deserts are greate,

KING: You wrong the honour of Nobilitie,
To place a robber in a Barons stead,   2845

QUEENE: Its well ye tearme him not a murtherer.

KING: Had I mistearmed him?

QUEENE: I that had you Henry.
He did a a peece of Justice at my Bidding.

KING: Who made you a Justice?

HENRY: I that had the power.

KING: You had none then.   2850

                    ¶Enter GLOSTER and SKINKE.

LEYSTER: Yes he was crowned before.

HENRY: Why does not Gloster weare a Coronet?

GLOSTER: Because his Soveraigne doth not weare a Crowne.

HENRY: By heaven put on thy Coronet, or that heaven   2855
Which now with a clear [eye], lends us this light,
Shall not be courtain'd with the vaile of night,
Eare on thy head I clap a burning Crowne,
Of red hot Yron that shall seare thy braines.

RICHARD: Good Gloster crowne thee with thy Coronet.   2860

LANCASTER: Doo gentle Earle.

SKINKE: Swounds doo, would I had one.

QUEENE: Doo not I prethee keepe thy proude heart still.

GLOSTER: Ile weare it but to crosse thy froward will.

HENRY: Sit downe and take thy place.

GLOSTER: Its the low earth,
To her I must, from her I had my breath.   2865

HENRY: We are pleas'd thou shalt sit there, Skinke take thy
                                              [place
Among my nobles.

[K4]   ¶Enter JOHN and ISABELL with Coronets.

SKINKE: Thankes to King Henries grace,

JOHN: John Earle of Morton and of Nottingham,   2870
With Isabell his Countesse, bow themselves
Before their brother Henries Royall Throane.

HENRY: Assend your seates, live in our daily love.

                ¶Enter RICHARD and ROBERT with Coronets.

RICHARD: Richard the Prince of England, with his Ward   2875
The noble Robert Hood, Earle Huntington,
Present their service to your Majestie.

HENRY: Y'are welcome too, though little be your love.

¶Enter FAUKENBRIDGE with his LADY, she a Coronet.

FAUKENBRIDGE: Olde Richard Faukenbridge, Knight of the
                                                    [crosse,
Lord of the Cinque ports, with his noble wife   2881
Dame Marrian Countesse of west Hereford,
Offer their duties at this Royall meeting.

HENRY: Sit downe, thou art a newter, she a foe,
Thy love we doubt, her hart too well we know.   2885
What suters are without, let them come in.

GLOSTER: And have no Justice where contempt is King.

HENRY: Mad man I give no eare to thy loose words.

JOHN: O sir y'are welcome, you have your old seat.

GLOSTER: Though thou sit hier yet my heart's as great.   2890

QUEENE: Great heart we'll make you lesser by the head.

GLOSTER: Ill comes not ever to the threatned.

                    ¶Enter BLOCKE and REDCAP.

HENRY: What are you two?

REDCAP: M ma mary and't please you I am Re Re Redcap.   2895

HENRY: And what's your mate?

BLOCKE: A poore Porter sir.

JOHN: The Porter of the fleet that was condemned.

BLOCKE: No truely sir I was Porter last, when I left the doore
open at the Taverne.

JOHN: O ist your sir?

LEYSTER: And what would you two have?   2900

REDCAP: I co co come to re re re qui quier the young K K King
of his go goo goodnes, since Glo Gloster is t taken, that he
wo wo would let my fa fa father have his pa pa pardon.

[K4^V] HENRY: Sirra yuour father has his pardon sign'd,
Go to the office it shall be delivered.   2905

REDCAP: And shall he be P P Porter a ga gaine?

HENRY: I that he shall, but let him be advis'd
Heareafter, how he lets out prisoners.

REDCAP: I wa warrant ye my Lord.

HENRY: What hast thou more to say?   2910

REDCAP: Marry I wo would have Skinke pu punisht for co co
cunnicatching me.

LEYSTER: Is that your busines?

REDCAP: I by my t t troth is it.

HENRY: Then get away.   2915

GLOSTER: Against Skinke (poore knave) thou gets no right
                                        [this day.
BLOCKE: O but run backe Redcap for the Pursevant.

REDCAP: O I Lord s sir, I have another s sute for the P P
Pursevant, that has l l lost his b b box, and his wa wa
warrant,   2920

HENRY: What meanes the fellow?

REDCAP: Why the Pu Pu Pursevant sir and the Po Po Porter.

GLOSTER: The box that I had from him, there it is.

FAUKENBRIDGE: Mary a me, and I was chargd with it.
Had you it brother Gloster? Gods good mercy,   2925

HENRY: And what have you to say?

BLOCKE: Nothing sir but God bless you, you are a goodly
company, except sir Richard or my Lady wil command me any more
service.   2929

FAUKENBRIDGE: Away you prating knave, hence varlet, hence.

                    ¶Exit.

LEYSTER: Put forth them fellowes there.

REDCAP: A f fo fore I go goe I b b be s s seech you let Sk
Skinke and Gl Gloster be lo lo looked too, for they have p p
playd the k k knaves to to to b b bad.   2935

HENRY: Take hence that stuttering fellow, shut them forth.

REDCAP: Nay Ile ru ru run, faith you shall not n n need to b b

b bid him ta ta take m me away, for Re Re Redcap will r ru run
rarely.   ¶EXIT.

HENRY: The sundrie misdemeanors late committed,   2940
As theftes and shifts in other mens disguise,
We now must (knave Skinke) freely tell thy faults.

[L]   SKINKE: Sweet King by these two terrors to myne enemies, that
lend light to my bodies darknes: Cavilero Skinke being 2944
beleagerd with an hoste of leaden heeles, arm'd in ring Irish:
cheated   my stammerer of his Red cap and Coate; was surprised,
brought to the fleet as a person suspected, past currant, till
Gloster   stript me from my counterfet, clad my backe in silke
and my hart in sorrow, and so left me to the mercy of my
mother witt: how Prince John releast me, he knowes: howe 2950
I got Faukenbridges chaine, I know: but how he will get it
againe, I know not.

FAUKENBRIDGE: Where is it sirra, tell me where it is?

GLOSTER: I got it from him, and I got Johns sword,

JOHN: I would twere to the hilts up in thy harte.   2955

RICHARD: O be more charitable brother John.

LEYSTER: My Leidge, you need not by perticulars
Examine what the world knows too plaine,
If you will pardon Skinke, his life is sav'd.
If not, he is convicted by the Law.   2960
For Gloster: as you worthyly resolv'd,
First take his hand, and afterward his head.

HENRY: Skinke thou hast life, our pardon and our love.

SKINKE: And your forgiveness for my robbery?

JOHN: Tut never trouble me with such a toy.   2965
Thou hindrest me from hearing of my joye.

HENRY: Bring forth a blocke, wine, water and towell,
Knives, and a Surgion to binde up the vaines,
Of Glosters arme: when his right hand is off,
His hand that strooke Skinke at the Parlament: 2970

SKINKE: I shall beare his blowes to my grave my Lord.

KING: Sonne Henry see thy fathers palzie hands,
Joyn'd like two supplyants, pressing to thy throwne?
Looke how the furrowes of his aged cheeke,
Fild with the revolets of wet eyde mone,   2975
Begs mercy for Earle Gloster? weigh his gilt,

Why for a slave, should Royall blood be spilt?

SKINKE: You wrong myne honour: Skinke may be reveng'd,

HENRY: Father I doe commend your humble course.
[L^v]   But quite dislike the project of your sute.   2980
Good words in an ill cause makes the fact worse,
Of blood or Basenes, Justice will dispute,
The greater man the greater his transgression,
Where strength wrongs weaknes, it is meare oppression,

LADY: O but King Henry heare a sister speake,   2985
Gloster was wrong'd, his lands were given away,
They are not Justly said, Just lawes to break,
That keep their owne right, with what power they may,
Thinke then thy Royall selfe began the wrong,
In giving Skinke what did to him belong.   2990

QUEENE: Heare me Sonne Henry, while thou art a King,
Give, take, pryson, thy subjects are thy slaves,
Lift meek to thrones: proud hearts in dungions fling.
Grace men today, to morrowe give them graves.
A King must be like Fortune; ever turning,   2995
The world his football, all her glory spurning.

GLOSTER: Still your olde counsaile Beldam pollicie,
You'r a fit Tutresse in a Monarchy.

RICHARD: Mother you are unjust, savage, too cruell,
Unlike a woman: gentlenes guides their sexe,   3000
But you to furyes fire ad more fewell,
The vexed spirit will you delight to vex?
O God when I consaite what you have done,
I am a sham'd to be esteem'd your sonne.

JOHN: Base Richard, I disdaine to call thee brother,   3005
Takest thou a traytors part in our disgrace?
For Gloster, wilt thou wrong our sacred mother?
I scorne thee and defie thee to thy face.
O that we were in field, then shouldst thou trie.

ROBERT: How fast Earle John would from Prince Richard flye
Thou meet a Lyon in feeld? poor mouse,   3011
All thy Carreers are in a Brothell house.

JOHN: Zounds boy.

RICHARD: Now man:

LEYSTER: Richard you wrong Prince John.

RICHARD: Leyster tweare Good you proov'd his Champion.

[L2]   JOHN: Hasten the execution Royall Lord,   3015
        Let deeds make answer for their worthlesse wordes.

        GLOSTER: I know if I respected hand or head,
        I am encompassed with a world of frends,
        And could from fury bee delivered.
        But then my freedom hazards many lives.   3020
        Henry performe the utmost of thy hate,
        Let thy hard harted mother have her wil,
        Give Franticke John no longer cause to prate,
        I am prepared for the worst of ill,
        You see my knees kisse the could pavements face,   3025
        They are not bent to Henry or his frends,
        But to all you whose bloud fled to your hearts,
        Shewes your true sorrowe in your ashye cheekes:
        To you I bend my knees, you I intreat,
        To smile on Glosters Resolution.   3030
        Who ever loves me will not shed a teare,
        Nor breath a sigh, nor show a cloudy frowne,
        Looke Henry, heares my hand, I lay it downe,
        And sweare as I have Knighthood heer't shall lye,
        Till thou have used all thy tyranny.   3035

        LADY: Has no man heart to speake?

        GLOSTER: Let all that love me
        Keepe silence, or by heaven Ile hate them dying.

        QUEENE: Harry off with his hand, then with his head.

        FAUKENBRIDGE: By the red rood I cannot chuse but weepe.
        Come love or hate my teares I cannot keepe.   3040

        QUEENE: When comes this lingring executioner?

        JOHN: An executioner: an executioner:

        HENRY: Call none til we have drunke: father fill wine,
        To day your Office is to beare our cupp.

        RICHARD: Ile fill it Henry.   ¶KING KNEELE DOWNE.

        HENRY: Dicke you are too meane,   3045
        So bow unto your soveraigne, Gloster learne:

        GLOSTER: Kneele to his childe? O hell! O tortor!
        Who would love life, to see this huge dishonor?

        HENRY: Saturne kneel'd to his Sonne, the God was faine
        To call young Jove his ages Soveraigne.   3050
[L2ᵛ]   Take now your seate againe and weare your Crowne;

Now shineth Henry like the Middayes Sonne,
Through his Horizon, darting all his beames,
Blinding with his bright splendor every eye,
That stares against his face of Majesty.   3055
The Commets, whose malicious gleames
Threatned the ruyne of our Royalty,
Stands at our mercy, yet our wrath denyes
All favour, but extreame extreamityes
Gloster, have to thy sorrow, chafe thy arme   3060
That I may see thy bloud (I long'd for oft)
Gush from thy vaines, and staine this Pallace roofe.

JOHN: Twould exceed gilding.

QUEENE: I as golde doth Oaker.

GLOSTER: Its wel ye count my bloud so precious.

HENRY: Leyster reach Gloster wine.

LEYSTER: I reach it him?   3065

HENRY: Proude Earle ile spurne thee, quickely goe and beare
[it.

GLOSTER: Ile count it poyson if his hand come neere it.

HENRY: Give it him Leyster upon our displeasure.

GLOSTER: Thus Gloster takes it, thus againe he flings it,
In scorne of him that sent it, and of him that [brings] it.

SKINKE: O brave spirit!   3071

LADY: Bravely resolv'd brother, I honour thee.

QUEENE: Harke how his sister joyes in his abuse?
Wilt thou endure it Hall?

FAUKENBRIDGE: Peace good Marian.

HENRY: Avoyde there every under Officer.   3075
Leave but us, our Pieres and Ladyes heere.
Richard you love Earle Gloster: looke about
If you can spye one in this company,
That hath done as great a sinne as Gloster;
Chuse him, let him be the executioner.   3080

RICHARD: Thou hast done worse then, like rebellious head,
Hast arm'd ten thousand hands against his life
That lov'd thee so, as thou wert made a King,
Being his childe, now he's thy underling.

[L3] I have done worse: thrise I drew my swoord,   3085
      In three set battles for thy false defence.
      John hath done worse, he still hath tooke thy part,
      All of us three have smitte our fathers heart;
      Which made proude Leyster bolde to strike his face,
      To his eternall shame, and our disgrace.   3090

      HENRY: Silence, I see thou meanst to finde none fit.
      I am sure, nor Lancaster, nor Huntington,
      Nor Faukenbridge, will lay a hand on him.
      Mother, wife, brother, lets descend the Throane
      Where Henry as the Monarch of the West,   3095
      Hath set amongst his Princes dignified.
      Father take you the place, see Justice done.

      KING: Its unjust Justice I must tell thee Sonne.

      HENRY: Mother holde you the Bason, you the Towell,
      I know your French hearts thirst for English bloud; 3100
      John, take the Mallet, I will holde the knife,
      And when I bid thee smite, strike for thy life:
      Make a marke Surgion, Gloster now prepare thee.

      GLOSTER: Tut, I am ready, to thy worst I dare thee.

      HENRY: Then have I done my worst, thrise honoured Earle, 3105
      I doe embrace thee in affections armes.

      QUEENE: What meanes thou Henry? O what meanes my Son?

      HENRY: I meane no longer to be lullaby'd,
      In your seditious armes.

      HENRY'S WIFE: MORDIEU Henry.

      HENRY: MORDIEU nor devill, little tit of Fraunce,   3110
      I know your hart leapes, at our hearts mischaunce.

      JOHN: Swounds Henry thou art mad:

      HENRY: I have bin mad;
      What stampst thou John? knowst thou not who I am?
      Come stamp the devill out, suckt from thy Dam.

      QUEENE: Ile cursse thee Henry.

      HENRY: You'r best be quiet,   3115
      Least where we finde you, to the Tower we beare yee,
      For being abroad England hath cause to feare yee.

      KING: I am strucke dombe with wonder.

[L3^V] GLOSTER: I amaz'd,
          Imagine that I see a vizion.   3119

          HENRY: Gloster, I give thee first this Skinke, this slave,
          Its in thy power, his life to spill or save,

          SKINKE: He's a noble gentleman, I doe not doubt his usage.

          HENRY: Stand not thus wondring, Princes kneele all downe,
          And cast your Coronets before his Crowne.
          Downe stubborne Queene, kneele to your wronged King,   3125
          Downe Mammet; Leyster Ile cut off thy legs,
          If thou delay thy duety: when proude John?

          JOHN: Nay if all kneele, of force I must be one.

          FAUKENBRIDGE: Now by my holydom a vertuous deed.

          HENRY: Father you see your most rebellious sonne,   3130
          Stricken with horror of his horred guilt,
          Requesting sentence fitting his desart,
          O treade upon his heade, that trode your heart.
          I doe deliver up all dignity,
          Crowne, Scepter, swoord, unto your Majesty.   3135

          KING: My heart surfets with joy in hearing this.
          And deare Sonne ile blesse thee with a kisse.

          HENRY: I will not rise, I will not leave this ground,
          Till all these voyces joyned in one sound:
          Cry, God save Henry second of that name,   3140
          Let his friends live, his foes see death with shame.

          ALL: God save Henry second of that name,
          Let his friends live, his foes see death with shame.

          HENRY: Amen, Amen, Amen.

          JOHN: Harke mother harke?
          My brother is already turned Clarke.   3145

          QUEENE: He is a recreant, I am mad with rage.

          HENRY: Be angry at your envy gracious mother,
          Learne patience and true humility
          Of your worst tuter'd Sonne, for I am he,
          Send hence that Frenchwoman, give her her dowry,   3150
          Let her not speake, to trouble my milde soule,
          Which of this world hath taken her last leave:
          And by her power, will my proude flesh controule.
          Off with these silkes, my garments shall be gray,
[L4]   My shirt hard hayre, my bed the ashey dust,   3155

My pillow but a lumpe of hardned clay:
For clay I am, and unto clay I must,
O I beseech ye let me goe alone,
To live, where my loose life I may bemone.

KING: Sonne?

QUEENE: Sonne?

RICHARD: Brother?

JOHN: Brother?

HENRY: Let none   3160
Call me their Sonne, I am no mans brother,
My kindred is in heaven, I know no other,
Farewell, farewell, the world is yours, pray take it.
Ile leave vexation, and with joy forsake it.   ¶EXIT.

LADY: Wondrous conversion.

FAUKENBRIDGE: Admirable good: 3165
Now by my holydam Mall passing good.

RICHARD: H'ath fir'd my soule I will to Palestine,
And pay my vowes before the Sepulcher,
Among the multitude of misbeliefe.
Ile shew my selfe the Souldier of Christ,   3170
Spend bloud, sweat teares, for satisfaction
Of many many sinnes which I lament:
And never thinke to have them pardoned,
Till I have part of Sirria conquered.

GLOSTER: He makes me wonder, and inflames my spirits,   3175
With an exceeding zeale to Portingale,
Which Kingdome the unchristned Sarisons,
The blacke fac'd Affricans, and tawny Moores,
Have got unjustly in possession:
Whence I will fire them with the help of heaven.   3180

SKINKE: Skinke will scortch them brave Gloster
Make Carbonadoes of their Bacon fletches;
Deserve to be counted valiant by his valour,
And Ryvo will he cry, and Castile too,
And wonders in the land of Civile doo.   3185

ROBERT: O that I were a man to see these fights,
To spend my bloud amongst these worthy Knights.

FAUKENBRIDGE: Mary aye me, were I a boy againe,
[L4^V] Ide either to Jerusalem or Spaine.

JOHN: Faith Ile keepe England, mother you and I   3190
Will live, for all this fight and foolery.

KING: Peace to us all, let's all for peace give prayse,
Unlookt for peace, unlookt for happy dayes,
Love Henries birth day, he hath bin new borne,
I am new crown'd, new settled in my seate.   3195
Let's all to the Chappell, there give thankes and praise,
Beseeching grace from Heavens eternal Throne,
That England never know more Prince then one.   ¶EXEUNT.

Finis.

Explanatory Notes

IN THOSE OF THE FOLLOWING notes which are merely glosses I have generally not glossed words which differ only in spelling from their modern equivalents, such as "foorth" (= forth); "stolne" (= stolen); "Coossen" (=cousin); and so forth. Except where some other source is noted, I have relied on the OXFORD ENGLISH DICTIONARY (Oxford, 1928, suppl. 1933), but I have only given those definitions as are indicated by the use of the word in LOOKE ABOUT YOU.

LINE

4 lighted] alighted, dismounted.

9 crosse high-way] crossroad.

13 Orizons] prayers.

20 speed] success.

21 meede] merit.

35 Rosamond] "Fair Rosamond," Rosamond Clifford, Henry II's mistress. See Introduction, pp. xvi-xvii, and Vergil B. Heltzel, FAIR ROSAMOND: A STUDY OF THE DEVELOPMENT OF A LITERARY THEME (Evanston, 1947).

42 benizon] blessing.

46 keep] in the sense of "keep to the house."

51 poast] send quickly, as in post-haste.
   incontinent] at once.

58 Hugh the Cryer] Among the announcements the town crier had to make were charges aganist fugitive criminals.

76 queane] slut, whore.

83 girt] dressed, arrayed.

94 brother John] in the sense of kinsman or fellow prince, since Gloster is a royal bastard.

95 Thy brother?] John is here disclaiming any kinship with John, either because Gloster is illegitimate, or because they are enemies, and there can thus be no "brother-hood" between them in the more general sense of the word.

100 releasement of the Queene] Queen Elinor (of Aquitaine), consort to Henry II, had been imprisoned after the death of Rosamond, in which the king considered to have been implicated. See Introduction, pp. xvi-xvii.

102 Bohmine Earle of Leister] As Mrs. Lancashire points out (p. 160), the surname of the Earls of Leicester in this period was Beaumont. "Bohmine" may be a corruption of Beaumont, or may suggest some confusion between the Beaumont and Bohun families. Humphrey III de Bohun (d. 1187) was a supporter of Henry II, and opposed Robert Beaumont, second Earl of Leicester. (See DNB).

112 head] group.

116 hollow of newes-thirsting eares] Perhaps an echo of ROMEO AND JULIET III. v. 2-3: "pierced the fearful hollow of thine ear."

119 Cliffords daughters death] i.e. Rosamond's death. See note to 1. 100 above.

148, 150-51] These are references to the wars fought between Henry II and his sons in parts of the Angevin territories in France during 1173-74, in which the Queen openly supported her sons. (See Holinshed for the years 1173-74, and Anne B. Lancashire, "LOOK ABOUT YOU as a History Play," SEL IX, 2 (Spring 1969), 321-34.)

149 Northerne borders] While Henry II was busy putting down the rebellion of his sons in 1173-74, William of Scotland took the opportunity to invade England and do considerable damage, though he was ultimately defeated and captured. Lancaster is here suggesting that the invasion was ultimately Elinor's fault, and in any case certainly not Rosamond's.

179 quite] requite, repay.

187 bower] bedchamber, boudoir.
    Stepney] then a village east of London where Faukenbridge lives, now part of Greater London.

191 it's ill to halt before the lame.] it's difficult to pretend to be a cripple in front of a real one; i.e. being

just as wanton as you are, I can see what you're up to.

197 The Provinces that lye beyond the Seas] the English lands in France.

198 the Isles that compasse in the mayne] the offshore islands, e.g. Isle of Wight, Isle of Man, Anglesey, etc.

210 And yet not give his sonnes such maintenaunce] Holinshed mentions this grievance (II, 148); see Introduction, p. xiv; and Lancashire article, p. 324.

215 as Jeffrey is a Duke] a reference to their elder brother Geoffrey, Duke of Brittany (d. 1185), who does not appear in the present play.

233 Entred a laborinth to murther love] Elinor was supposed to have followed Henry to Rosamond's bower (enclosed within a maze or labyrinth for greater safety), and after he had left, entered herself and either poisoned Rosamond, or, as LOOKE ABOUT YOU renders the legend, had a hired assassin (Skinke) do so. See Heltzel, FAIR ROSAMOND, passim.

240 For glorious is the sway of Majesty] Perhaps an echo (or parody, since it comes from John) of Tamburlaine's lines in Marlowe's TAMBURLAINE, Part I (in COMPLETE PLAYS OF CHRISTOPHER MARLOWE, ed. Irving Ribner [New York, 1963], (II. v. 51, 53-4):

TAMBURLAINE: Is it not passing brave to be a king, Techelles?
Is it not passing brave to be a king,
And ride in triumph through Persepolis?

and is particularly ironical here, since King Henry is hardly very glorious or very majestic in this scene.

247-252] References to Richard's intended participation in the Third Crusade.

257 well a neere] alas. According to the OED, this is the earliest use of this expression, which it considers a probable variation of "welladay," as Lancashire points out (p. 180).

259 Brother] They are brothers-in-law.

261 You shall not stand to this?] Will you agree to this?

272 Otimie] atomy, a tiny thing, a pigmy.

281 billes] a long pole-weapon, with an axe at the end.

296 indifferent] impartial.

300 affect] like, as in affection.

306 I have had wrong about his wardship.] A somewhat ambiguous line. Does Henry mean that he has heard of some (unmentioned) abuse of Richard's rights of wardship over Huntington, or does he mean that he himself has been wronged by the decision to give the lucrative wardship to Richard rather to himself as elder brother? In any case the complaint helps to define his character in the play.

310 bill] petition or complaint.

332 Rowden Lordship] Either Roden in Shropshire (see R. W. Eyton, ANTIQUITIES OF SHROPSHIRE, VII [London, 1858], 373), or Rowden in Leicestershire. (See J. H. F. Brabner, ed., THE COMPREHENSIVE GAZETEER OF ENGLAND AND WALES [London, 1895], s.v. Rowden; and Mrs. Lancashire's dissertation, p. 190, to which I am indebted for this note.

333 my lands] No historical evidence has been found proving that either Roden or Rowden ever formed part of the lands of the earldom of Gloucester; but if one of them did, it was more likely to have been Roden in Shropshire, since the Gloucester lands lay mainly in the west and southwest (see THE CAMBRIDGE MEDIEVAL HISTORY ed. J. R. Tanner, et al. Vol. V., pp. 536-7.)

342 parts] a conflict between or among several parties or groups, according to the OED, which considers the word a plural of part-fray, and quotes this line.
      Swonds] 'swounds, an oath ("by God's wounds," one of a fairly extensive group: e.g. 'sblood; 'sbones; etc.)

357 poasts] quick messengers, presumably armed; see note to line 51 above.

359 Liefetenant of the Tower] the chief officer of the Tower of London, the oldest and most important of the London prisons, generally reserved for noble or royal prisoners accused or suspected of high treason. The Lieutenant of the Tower was an important government official, often of knight's rank, as is Sir Robert Brakenbury, for example, in Shakespeare's RICHARD III. Though until a fairly late date the Tower was also a royal palace and armoury, confinement in the Tower was a serious matter, which is why the King prefers that Gloster should be sent to the Fleet instead.

369 Warden of th' Fleete] The Fleet was a prison generally reserved for "'those that act or speak anything in contempt of the Courts of Chancery and Common Pleas,' and was used mostly for the detention of persons convicted by the Star Chamber." (See William Newton, LONDON IN THE OLDEN TIME [London, 1855],

p. 82; and Mrs. Lancashire's dissertation, p. 196, to which I am indebted for the first part of this note.) The Warden was the chief officer of the prison, which stood in what is now Fleet Street.

379 Redcap] This was perhaps a generic name for all message-carriers, baggage-handlers, and the like, then as now. But Professor Lancashire notes (p. 142) that in both English and Germanifold tradition a red cap is the mark of a goblin or elf.

Tipstaffe] a bailiff or constable attached to a court, from the metal-tipped staff he carried as a mark of office.

404 Thou lookest like love] i.e like Cupid, the god of love, usually portrayed as a boy with a bow -- particularly appropriate if it is remembered that Huntington will grow up to be Robin Hood, the archer of Sherwood.

419 It was not well done heere] i.e in the royal presence, and in Parliament.

432 Fort of Bungye] "Bungay Castle, situated in Suffolk on a deep bend of the river Waveney, was in the twelfth century the stronghold of the Bigods, Earls of Norfolk. Hugh Bigod, who supported the Young King and his brothers against their father, is reported to have defied Henry II and to have boasted:

> Were I in my castle of Bungay,
> Upon the river of Waveney,
> I would ne care for the King of Cockney.

This boast became the subject of a ballad (see THE SUFFOLK GARLAND [Ipswich, 1818], pp. 137-139) and eventually a proverb (see M. P. Tilley, A DICTIONARY OF THE PROVERBS IN ENGLAND IN THE SIXTEENTH AND SEVENTEENTH CENTURIES [Ann Arbor, 1950], C123). The author of LOOKE ABOUT YOU has transferred to Gloster both Bungay Castle and Bigod's famous boast. See John Wodderspoon, HISTORIC SITES ... IN THE COUNTY OF SUFFOLK (London, 1839), pp. 229-32; THE SUFFOLK GARLAND (as above); and Holinshed, II, 328 (boast wrongly dated in the reign of Henry III).

I am indebted to Mrs. Lancashire's dissertation for this note, which I have quoted in full since I do not think it can be bettered.

441 wight] men (singular or plural).

442 Keeps] common form in 16th C. grammar; see E. A. Abbott, SHAKESPEAREAN GRAMMAR, 3rd ed. (New York, 1870), no. 333.

453 the commons feare] i.e. your fear of what the commons would do.

454 Keep your State Lords] Don't let our departure break up your procession -- perhaps as strong as "don't bother getting up."

461 Blacke Heath] a large tract of open land across the Thames some four or five miles from London, a place frequented by highwaymen.
       and] (or an) if, especially in colloquial speech.
       King of all Kent] Blacke Heath was then a part of Kent, though it is now part of Greater London.

464-469] Skinke is here describing his flight from Westminster through London, to Stepney on the east, where he meets Redcap, and where he hopes to find a boat to take him across the Thames to Kent where his Hermit's cave (and safety) are. As he movingly expresses it (1. 468-9): "O Kent, O Kent, I would give my part of all Christendome to feele thee as I see thee."

507 Gravesend at the Angell] Gravesend is a port on the Thames about 27 miles below London; the Angel was presumably a tavern there. Since Skinke has no intention of meeting Redcap there, the name of the tavern may be his quick invention.

514 Ile give the turning of the key for nothing] I'll let you out without a bribe.

527 Pyanet] magpie-like, i.e. chattering.

529 tytty tytty a the tongue I beleeve will faile mee] I don't think I can imitate stammering well enough to pass the guards.

532 make up to] go up to.

536 sirra] a condescending form of address to boys, and one's (male) social inferiors.

553 nobilitie in reversion] Though Robert bears the title Earl of Huntington, he is still a minor, his property and its income being held by his guardian, Prince Richard. Thus Robert only owns them "in reversion," at such time as he comes of age, the grant of wardship to Richard therefore expires, and the property reverts to Robert. (Blocke is teasing him.)

555-56 swearing to the pantable] The frequently mentioned supposed privilege of a page to administer an oath on a pantable (or more frequently pantofle, a slipper) seems most clearly explained in Thomas Nashe's THE UNFORTUNATE TRAVELER (London: Thomas Scarlet for Cuthbert Burby, 1594; STC 18381) A2v:
       "...whereas you [pages] were wont to swere men on a

pantofle to be true to your puisant [mighty] order, you shall
sweare them on nothing but this chronicle of the king of Pages
hence forward."
          Clearly it was a kind of game or joke on those at court
who were inferior even to the pages, (or by older pages on
younger ones).

557 cutting of tagges] Tags were laces, which held up a
gentleman's hose, so that when the tags were cut the hose fell
down, no doubt to the vast amusement of everyone present
except the wearer.

557-8 CUM MULTIS ALIIS] with many others, a Latin tag.

574 conjure his gaberdine] A gaberdine was a long cloak made
of rough material, which he pictures grief as wearing; conjure
here seems to mean get rid of as if by conjuration.

607 misconster] misconstrue, misunderstand.

624 beadroll] a long list, figuratively, a large number, from
the pre-Reformation lists of the dead for whose souls a
beadsman was to pray.

642 ca ca ca ca] imitating Skinke's imitation of Redcap's
stammer, which he likens to the caw-ing of the jackdaw (see
ll. 946 and 959 below.)

647 crowne] a coin worth five shillings.

654 buttery bar] The buttery was (and still is, in Cambridge
colleges) the place where food and drink were stored and
dispensed to the household. The buttery bar was the dutch-door
over which the requested items were dispensed.
     stitty stitty] a nonce-word, according to the OED, which
defines it as "a derisive epithet applied to a stammerer," and
quotes this line as the only occurrence.

656 trylill] "with the sound of flowing liquor," according to
the OED, which cites this line.

659 LUPUS IN FABULA] "[Here's] the wolf in the fable;" or as
Lancashire suggests (p. 240): "Speak of the wolf and he will
appear."

669 sconce] head

673-4] Blocke somewhat jocularly advises Faukenbridge to try a
sallet (salad) of parsley, which represented a hot, dry humor,
to counteract the cold, wet humor of his old body, along with
the herb patience, which Mrs. Lancashire suggests Blocke may
mention solely for its name, but which, as she points out,

also was thought useful in treating diseases "proceeding of
cold causes." See William Turner, THE FIRST AND SECONDE PARTES
OF THE HERBAL OF WILLIAM TURNER (London, 1568), I, p. 55;
Thomas Newton, THE OLDE MANS DIETARIE (London, 1586), sigs.
B4, C4v, C5v, C7v; John Gerard, HERBALL, ed. M. Woodward
(London, 1927), pp. 99-101; and Mrs. Lancashire's
dissertation, pp. 242, 244, to which I am indebted for this
note.

681] tines] horns, here the horns of the cuckold.

693] dead] here in the sense of profound, absolute.

708 spring] in the sense, apparently, of trick, and if so,
then the earliest recorded usage, since the OED lists none
before 1753.

719 And your cap too sir.] Hazlitt suggests that Blocke's
reference may be to an invisible cap from under which
Faukenbridge has been making his long series of asides, but
Mrs. Lancashire is probably correct in thinking that the
reference is to the fool's cap that Blocke thinks Faukenbridge
should be wearing.

743-4 Huntington's right heyre / His father Gilbert] As Mrs.
Lancashire points out (p. 254), Robin Hood's father is named
in no other version of the legend before 1600; though in the
DOWNFALL OF ROBERT EARL OF HUNTINGTON (1598), p. 108 and 169,
Robert's uncle, the Prior of York, is called Gilbert.
     smoothst fac'd] most clean-shaven, handsomest, best
looking (a trait which he has passed on to his son, and which
helps to confirm the rightness of the lineage mentioned in the
line before.)

751 Lidger] agent

758 toyes] trifles, but perhaps also a reference to
Huntington's youth, which Lady Faukenbridge may feel might
better be spent playing with toys than acting as go-between in
Richard's illicit suit.

760-765] Robert is here flirting with Lady Faukenbridge in a
rather grown-up way; at "You see I am weapn'd" he no doubt
indicates a dagger or short sword, but possibly also the large
padded codpiece characteristic of male attire of the period,
which would add another meaning to "stab" in the next line.

784 lyther] lazy, sluggish, according to the OED, which quotes
this line.

786 pye] chatterer, from magpie (see note to l. 527 above).

792 fadge] work, succeed.

807 Angels] (originally Angel-nobles) English gold coins with
an image of the Archangel Michael on one side, used somewhat
anachronistically is this play, since they were introduced
only under Edward IV in 1465, at which time their value was
six shillings eightpence.

818 cashyre your selfe] dismiss yourself, i.e. give up your
coat of office.

821 familliar] probably in the sense of the noun, familiar
spirit, devil, thus suggesting in the next line that Skinke
plays the black cat to Queen Elinor's witch; though as Mrs.
Lancashire points out (p. 264), the adjective, familiar in the
sense of affable, sociable, also makes sense, and must be
considered a possibility.

828 Mumbudgit] a command to be silent.

829 I mum mum faire, pray God may chaunce it] i.e. Yes, I'll
be quiet, very quiet, and may God prosper my escape as well as
yours. Perhaps also a pun on mumchance, a dice game.

840 trice] moment, i.e. a very short time.

851 bedry'd] dried up, i.e. silent.

852 caper hay] dance
    set all at six and seaven] (a dicing term), chance
everything on one throw.

857 Cousen Moorton] no specific relative of John's with the
name or title of Morton, Moorton, or Murton has been found.
    The earliest known ancestor of the present earls of Morton
(now in their twentieth generation) is one Sir Andrew Douglas,
who is known to have been alive in 1259, and therefore is
unlikely to have been connected with the events of the present
play.
    The situation is probably merely a contrivance to get John
to the prison so that Skinke can fool him and escape.

    See BURKE'S PEERAGE, BARONETAGE AND KNIGHTAGE (London,
1967), s.v. Morton.

858 morrow masse] early mass.

860 that preaching hate and prayer] i.e. those who hate
preaching and prayer.

862 bowles] As Mrs. Lancashire points out (p. 272), bowls was
a popular game among the aristocracy in the sixteenth and

seventeenth centuries, and was played at the Fleet, as we know from John Taylor, the water-poet:

Since Richards reigne the first, the Fleet hath beene
A prison, as upon records is seene:
For lodgings and for bowling, there's large space.

(See John Taylor, THE WORKS OF JOHN TAYLOR THE WATER-POET COMPRISED IN THE FOLIO EDITION OF 1630 (Spenser Society, 1869), p. 292, as quoted by Mrs. Lancashire, p. 272.)

873 the Jack] In the simplest form of the game of bowls, which John and Skinke seem to be playing here, the game begins when the first player throws the Jack, a small hard wooden ball, a certain distance onto the green as a target. He then launches his own bowl, a larger wooden ball which runs with a bias, the object being to run his bowl as close as possible to the Jack. Whichever player runs his closest to the Jack wins a point. The game (though in a more complex form in which each player has several bowls, and players are organized into teams) is still played in England today, and the present editor has played it many times on Christ's Pieces in Cambridge, though with what success need not be detailed here.

875 Rub, rub, rub, rub] The bowl is said to rub when it is slowed down by touching any object in its path; and John is here exhorting his bowl to slow down and not overshoot the Jack.

893] Keep my hat and cloak as security that I'll finish the game.

896 hey passe] a magician's "magic" word, the equivalent of abracadabra, exclaimed when he wants one object to turn into another. Skinke uses it here to accompany his change of disguise.

902 So.] all ready.

911 Drinke that] (giving him a tip.)

917 scrip] a traveler's or beggar's wallet.

930 practise] plot, subterfuge.

951 Midsomer] According to tradition, the midsummer moon was particularly conducive to lunacy.

960 sleveles tale] a trivial or feeble story, used here in the sense of a delaying device.

961 Newgate] the main municipal prison in London, where felons

and petty criminals were confined; distinct from both the Tower and the Fleet, where state criminals, generally of higher rank, were housed.

969 cony] rabbit. a cony-catcher was a trickster, a confidence man.

977 inhort] exhort, urge.

997 But ... hart-white] archery target; the hart-white was the white circle in the center, similar to the modern bull's eye.

998 rove] shoot at with arrows.

1000 upshot] the target.

1028 unkynd] unnatural, as well as the modern meaning of cruel.

1031 scarlet dyde] As Mrs. Lancashire points out, the King refers to scarlet as denoting cruelty and vengeance, while Henry means it to symbolize royalty and courage (p. 298).

1035 the Confessor] Edward the Confessor, King of England 1042-1066, much loved and respected as a religious man and merciful judge and lawgiver.

1041 He shall have lawe] He shall have the protection of the law.

1045-47 There was apparently a tradition, as Mrs. Lancashire points out (pp. 300, 582), that Robert Earl of Gloucester had led a crusade to Cadiz (Gads) in Spain and Sicily (Cicile) to free those places from Saracen rule, but there is no historical evidence to confirm it.

1049 a slave] i.e. Skinke.

1063 by my fay] by my faith, a very mild oath.

1068 Jack an apes] a foolish person, which John definitely feels after having been fooled by Skinke.

1069 Your monkey, your babone, your asse, your gull] all animals not known for their intelligence. The gull especially was a byword for stupidity (gullibility) and gave its name to the many easily cheated country folk who came to London each year. See Thomas Dekker, THE GULS HORNEBOOKE (London, for R. S[erger], 1609).

1072 Levarnian Lake] Lake Avernus, a dark and desolate lake near Naples, in Italy, often said to be an entrance to Hell.

See Vergil, AENEID, VI, 577-79.

1088-94] This speech is obviously patterned after Hotspur's famous speech in 1 HENRY IV (I. iii. 201-5), and the similarity between the two is a main point in Mrs. Lancashire's undoubtedly correct thesis that LOOKE ABOUT YOU is patterned on 1 HENRY IV; see Introduction, p. xv; and Lancashire dissertation, pp. 45-6.

1093 Briareus] The hundred-armed Titan whom Hesiod (Theog. 713-16) describes as helping the Olympian gods against his fellow Titans. In other versions of the legend, Briareus fights the Olympians himself, and this seems to be what is alluded to here.

1123 Pursevant] an official messenger of the Court.

1161 scarlet countenaunce] woman's complexion, perhaps referring to makeup.

1167 Peace] quiet.

1169 complaiment] ceremony.

1170 a bots on you] a curse; a bot is a maggot.

1184 By this] by this time

1189 dyeteth] nourishes, makes strong.

1190 Myrth ... spleane] The spleane was considered to be the center of mirth as well as of bad temper.

1191 furie!] i.e. mirth (personified).

1192 conceated] conceived, i.e. I am conceiving jests.

1193 a theeves hand] Gloster is offering his hand to Huntington, and likens himself to a thief. The humor lies in the audience being aware of Huntington's later career as the outlaw of Sherwood.

1200 Ha crake?] What, raven (or crow), both birds being considered bringer of ill omens or bad news, as Mrs. Lancashire points out (p. 322).

1257-8 noble...light / By the sixe shillings] Skinke is here punning on Noble, which was also the name of a gold coin, worth 6 shillings eightpence. He says his noble (humour) is light (undervalue) by six shillings, as we see it is in the next line, when he says that all he has is two groats, or eightpence.

1258 crackt] broken, unfit for circulation.

1259 helter skelter] throw away, waste.
     vawting house] =vaulting house =leaping house =brothel.

1268 iwis] certainly.

1282 set me under saile] set me up.

1294 exclaimes] i.e. the breath.

1304 geld] cut off part of it.

1353 By Thomas] By St. Thomas a Becket, Henry II's Archbishop of Canterbury, killed 29 December 1170, canonized February 1173. Whether or not anyone would be swearing by him so soon afer his death and/or canonization (the action of the play takes place 1173-74), it was a common oath in Elizabethan England.

1359 russet] reddish brown.

1374 Close] a reminder of "close watch" in line 1372.

1377-83] another speech reminiscent of Hotspur.

1384 proper] own.

1395 Drawers] barmen.

1395 Salutation] Mrs. Lancashire (p. 348) identifies this as a tavern on Newgate Street, London also mentioned in ARDEN OF FEVERSHAM (ed. C. F. Tucker Brooke, in THE SHAKESPEARE APOCRYPHA [Oxford, 1908]), III. iv. 25.

1412 shamelesse] as if it were John's name.

1415 princkocks] impertinent boy.

1450 Much follow you.] (not) much (chance I'll) follow you.

1446 Labandalashot, or rowe wel ye Marriners] the names of popular ballads. For seven different versions of "Rowe Well Ye Marynors" see H. E. Rollins, ed., AN ANALYTICAL INDEX TO THE BALLAD-ENTRIES IN THE STATIONERS REGISTER (Chapel Hill, 1924), p. 201.

1460 bare] not holding anything.

1470 Sacke] any of the various dry white wines from Spain or the Canary Islands popular in England in the 16th and 17th centuries; (from Fr. vin sec [dry wine.])

1472 Anan] (or Anon, the more usual form), i.e. be right there! Anon is the customary answer of the drawer in Elizabethan plays. See the very similar scene wih Francis the drawer in 1 HENRY IV (II. iv). Mrs. Lancashire points out (p. 358) that though the word is spelled anon everywhere else in LOOKE ABOUT YOU, in the two tavern scenes it is spelled anan, and concludes that it may be an attempt on the part of the author to give the Drawer a distinctive manner of speech.

1481 nippitate] strong, best.

1486 swound] swoon, faint.

1503 fashion] habit.

1504 falling sickenes] i.e. epilepsy; Mrs. Lancashire points out (p. 362) that wine was thought to aggravate this condition.

1507 boxe] dispatch-box, described later in 11. 1664-5.

1510 proteus] a changing or inconstant person or thing, from the Greek sea-god Proteus, who assumed various shapes.

1512 curres] dogs.

1523 Crowne] the names of one of the rooms in the tavern.

1527 dog'd] followed, "hounded" out.

1550 holberts] halberds, a combined spear and battle-axe.

1570 prentises] apprentices.

1581 waxeth] grows.

1596 fire of Saint Anthony] erysipelas, an acute infectious disease of the skin or mucous membrane, probably connected with Saint Anthony in the following way, as Mrs. Lancashire points out (p. 376), quoting a note on line 427 of "The Parson's Tale" in F. N. Robinson's edition of THE WORKS OF GEOFFREY CHAUCER (Boston, 1957), p. 769: "Mr. J. U. Nicolson (THE COMPLETE WORKS OF VILLON, tr. [New York, 1931], pp. 256ff) explains the name by the fact that the order of Saint Anthony in the Dauphine nursed the sick in an epidemic of the disease in the 13th [sic] century."

1601 copesmates] comrades.

1602-3 gesse...gesse] a play on the words guess and guests,

often spelt alike in the period.

1614 venterous] adventurous.

1631 posed] deposed, sworn.

1697 faine] desire.

1699 gibbet] gallows.

1700 Old Bayly] the criminal court, and apparently, place of execution for those in municipal prisons like Newgate. Later, at least by the eighteenth century, executions were performed at Tyburn.

1705 cousonage] cheating.

1723 Basiliske] a fabulous reptile which blasts objects by its glance.

1724 gleare ey'd] the OED lists this as a nonce-word; the meaning is probably glare-eyed, i.e. with glaring eyes, since John is apparently very self-consciously aware that everyone is looking at him after he angrily drives the suffering Pursevant out, and it further upsets him. But Mrs. Lancashire (p. 390) suggests that gleare may be a variant of "gleer," "gleering" meaning looking askance, or of "glair-eyed," meaning white-eyed, hence cowardly, since "glair" is the white of an egg.

1731 amaine] immediately.

1743 Cipria] Venus, goddess of earthly love.

1744 sea-borne mother] a reference to the tradition that Venus, goddess not only of love, but also of marriage and sexual fertility (hence motherhood), sprang from the sea foam.

1745 shine brightly] i.e. the planet Venus, the brightest planet in the solar system.

1771 Humphery] the servingman who entered at l. 1757. Sir Walter Greg, who edited the Malone Society reprint of LOOKE ABOUT YOU (1913), suggested that Humphery refers to Humphrey Ieffes, one of the actors of the Globe Theare company, who is called Humfrey in a stage direction in 3 HENRY VI. But as Mrs. Lancashire shows (p. 143), in this play the servant is called Humphery not once but several times, so that it must be the character's name, not the actor's.

1765 untrust] i.e. untrussed, out of hose and doublet, which

were connected by trusses or tags (see note to l. 557 above),
which supported the hose. Robert's point here is that he'll
never wear women's clothes again.

1776 lewd] silly.

1796 floute] tease, mock.

1798 use] continue.

1799 bob] strike, hit.

1800 beetle head] a mild insult; as Mrs. Lancashire points out
(p. 402), the beetle is proverbially dull or stupid.

1805 the Porters sonne, that was condemned] i.e. the son of
the porter that was condemned.

1812 Jaunts] journeys, here in the sense of hurried and
needless ones.

1821 have about] turn about, act other than kindly, i.e.
scold.

1824 'a] he.

1827 knicke a knocke] A nonce-word, according to the OED,
which calls it an "echoic word expressing a succession of
knocks of alternating character."

1842 Very sicke, sicke and like to dye] Mrs. Lancashire points
out (p. 406) that "Sick, sick, and very sick" is a common
ballad refrain, to which Blocke is alluding in "Ile sing it"
later in the line.

1843 and you wil.] if you wish.

1856 purchase] ill gotten gains.

1861 PAUCA VERBA] Lat., literally, few words; i.e. quiet!.

1873 As he beleeves] I hope she prove as unfaithful to him as
he believes her to be.

1878 honour'd] noble.

1887 anone] anon, soon.

1890 vouchsafe] condescend [to.]

1895 Raynald] Reynard, the name of the cunning fox in the
medieval beast fable REYNARD THE FOX.

1899 good custome] much business.

1918 graft ye] put horns on your head, i.e. make you a cuckold.

1940 Well by your leave sir Richard] It may be that, as Mrs. Lancashire believes, John takes the lady from Faukenbridge at this point, but I think it more likely that he merely interrupts their conversation and shows an interest in her, and, since Faukenbridge has already arranged a tryst with the lady, he is perfectly happy to leave her with John and pursue his talk with the hermit.

1941 free from feare] i.e. that his doings with the lady will get back to his wife.
     you'l melt, olde man] i.e. You're too old for hot stuff like this girl.

1942 shrow] shrew.

1954 sweeting] sweetheart.

1965 venter] venture, bet.

1969 Hinde] the name of the tavern near Faukenbridge's home at Stepney.

1970 Hinde...Roe] a hind is a female deer; John here seems to use roe to mean roebuck, the male of the roe species of deer in his play on words.

1973 Princesse] Princess Isabel, John's wife.

1988 meet with both of you] get even with you both.

2005 Faulconers lure] a lure for falcons, made of wood, with bits of plumage attached, which a falconer uses to call back the birds which he has sent after game.

2007 mouse] an affectionate term.

2011 trimme] cheat, here with the suggestion of seduce.
     Commodity] value, money.

2012 crownes] a pun on the two meanings of the word: 1) the English gold coin worth five shillings, and 2) the circlet of gold which a king wears on his head.

2018 portes] portable prayerbook.

2039 squatted] a hunter's term to describe an animal which is hiding in underbrush, but in this case referring to the thief.

2041 common wealths man] public-spirited citizen.

2044-2055 Staging Skinke's simultaneous robbery of John and Faukenbridge is somewhat difficult. Mrs. Lancashire suggests (p. 436) that perhaps they fall through trap doors into the caves mentioned in line 2042 above, but it seems more likely to the present editor that there is ground of some height between them, for example a rock or small hill, on which Skinke stands and threatens them both with his poniards (small daggers which could be used for throwing) after he has tripped John up.

2046 pate] head.

2058 fore-spoken at ye teate] doomed, damned, at his mother's breast, i.e. from the beginning.

2081 Ile faine] I would like to go

2083 od mate] other fellow.

2087 bum] hit.

2090 I am for him] I am ready for him.
    Robin Goodfellow] in English folklore, a mischievous elf or goblin thought to haunt the country-side; also known as Puck. See Shakespeare, MIDSUMMER-NIGHT'S DREAM.

2093 GENII] spirits.

2145 revile] revel.

2193 queristors] choristers.

2195 winged clarkes] i.e. birds (singing).

2212 had his peace] were at peace with everyone

2117 unblest] without last rites.

2227 raise power but we'l have peace] we'll have peace even if I have to raise an army to get it.

2233 speed] succeed.

2253 Lyne] lying.

2256 simply] plainly, referring to Richard's proposition.

2259 uncase] undress, change clothes.

2268 holde up] play along with.

2272 queane] slut, whore.

2274 Muttonmounger] whoremaster.

2294 passe my word] act as co-signer for a loan.

2298 decayde] become less prosperous, i.e. needs his money now.

2313 weare the yellow] be the jealous one, from the supposed custom of a jealous spouse wearing some yellow garment; for examples, see Mrs. Lancashire's dissertation, p. 470.

2315 curst] unpleasant.

2325 favour store] goodwill aplenty.

2335 peate] pet, sweetheart.

2341 dishclout] dishcloth.

2342 closet] a private room, perhaps his bedroom.
     earnest] first installment.

2352-2365 There is considerable confusion of speech-prefixes in this section of the text, as if the author himself became confused between the real Lady Faukenbridge, who is disguised as a merchant's wife, and the apparent Lady Faukenbridge, who is actually the boy Robin Hood in disguise. In l. 2352, therefore, it must be ROBERT, not LADY, who asks "Why speakst thou not, what aylst thou?" Likewise, at l. 2357, it must be ROBERT who tells BLOCKE to call in his fellows, for despite Mrs. Lancashire's claim that ROBERT is showing too much initiative in doing so, it would be giving up the whole game for LADY, who is supposed to be a merchant's wife, to presume to give orders in someone else's house, especially a countess's (see l. 2882 below, for Lady Faukenbridge's rank in her own right), let alone offer to "crack" their porter's "crowne" (l. 2358). Then, at l. 2365, the speech must be ROBERT's, since it concerns Faukenbridge's jealousy, and therefore must proceed from the mouth of his wife, who is being played by ROBERT. The only remaining problem is whom to assign l. 2355-6 "Ah olde cole...catcht." It seems more likely to the present editor that line 2355-6 belongs to ROBERT, who thus reacts to LADY's accusation against FAUKENBRIDGE, than to LADY herself, who does not need to ract to her own line, and who is, moreover, the center of attention after her accusation, and therefore not in the best position to utter a believable aside.

2353 rood] cross.

2355 cole] trickster, cheat, from dicing. As Mrs. Lancashire points out (p. 476),"a character in the morality play IMPATIENT POVERTY is named Cole Hazard, i.e., a cheater at dice, and Painted Profit is called Cole Profit in George Wapull's THE TIDE TARRIETH NO MAN (Tudor Facsimile Texts, 1910), sig. Diiii verso."

2372 The Constable for me] i.e. call him for me.

2375 drab] slattern, slut.

2376 bankrout] bankrupt.

2381 wert richer] if thou were richer.

2437 shift me] change my clothes.

2439 mattins] the morning service in the Anglican Book of Common Prayer, here used as a mild oath.

2479 quit] requited, paid back.

2484 verge] border, border country.

2496 bilbowe blade] i.e. made in Bilbao, Spain, famous for its fine steel.

2519 turn'd Livery] i.e. turncoat, with also the suggestion of then being so poorly treated as to have to wear his livery (uniform) inside-out rather than be bought a new one.

2537 foyle] repulse, setback.

2538 wreake] pain; loss of blood makes one thirsty.

2542 perry] wind.

2563 Gramercy] thank you.

2575 hie] speed.

2584 Cuz] short for cousin, here in the sense of kinsman, though royalty customarily address nobility in this manner.

2606 cudgell] a stout club.

2608 Znayles] an oath (by God's nails).

2615 caperclaw] beat.

2632 bumbast] beat.

2636 lid] eyelid, another oath.

2663 varlet] knave, lowborn criminal.

2722 ruth] grief.

2726 defend] forbid, as in "Defense de Fumer:" "Smoking is Forbidden."

2727 daine] deign, condescend to.

2762 gave me my hyre] what I deserved.

2765 guld] gulled, tricked.

2824 Sinet] sennet, flourish, fanfare.

2827 Globe] Orb, one of the marks of sovereignty.

2831 Coronets] small crowns worn by the nobility at solemn assemblies.

2835 Shew them our vize-roys] i.e. show them to be our viceroys, assistants or representatives of a king.

2841 Jouisanes] Fr., jouissance, enjoyment, pleasure.

2879 she a] i.e. she [wearing] a.

2881 Lord of the Cinque Ports] (today Lord Warden of the Cinque Ports), at one time the official in charge of a number of important seaports (originally five, hence cinque) on the south-eastern coast of England which furnished much of the Royal Navy. Formerly an important (and lucrative) position, it is now mainly ceremonial, and given to retired statesmen as an honor. Sir Winston Churchill held the office till his death in 1965.

2911 cunnicatching] cony-catching, cheating.

2930 prating] chattering.

2943-4 by these...darkenes] i.e. by my eyes.

2944 Cavilero] a self-styled title suggesting that Skinke sees himself as cavalier, free and easy, offhand.

2945 armed in ring Irish] a crux. Mrs. Lancashire suggests (p.

552) that ring-mail (i.e. chain mail) is meant; or that, since the Irish wore no armor in Elizabethan times, ring-Irish means no armor. But why mention it if they are not wearing any armor, particularly since Skinke is trying to emphasize the danger he was in?

2947 past currant] was accepted.

2987-8] These lines defy emendation. They seem to mean "they do not speak justly, who break just laws, and protect their own rights by force."

2997 Beldam] old lady.

3011 Lyon] Richard was known as Coeur-de-Lion.

3049 Saturne kneel'd to his Sonne] In Roman mythology, Saturn was deposed as king of the gods by his son Jove.

3052-58 These lines are reminiscent of the opening lines of Shakespeare's RICHARD III:
     Now is the winter of our discontent
     Made glorious summer by this son of York;
     And all the clouds that low'r'd upon our house
     In the deep bosom of the ocean buried.
quoted from THE RIVERSIDE SHAKESPEARE, ed. G. B. Evans (Boston, 1974).

3063 Oaker] ocher, a pale yellow clay.

3075 Avoyde] Leave, depart.

3109 MORDIEU] Fr., mort dieu, God's death, an oath.

3125 Mammet] a term of abuse.

3146 recreant] traitor, one who changes allegiance.

3182 Carbonadoes] pieces of broiled flesh.
     Bacon fletches] i.e. their sides (where bacon comes from.)

3184 Ryvo...Castile] exclamations used in drinking, and thought to come originally from the Spanish. For a detailed derivation, see Mrs. Lancashire's dissertation, p. 586.

3185 Civil] Seville, the part of Spain where the Moors were strongest.

Textual Notes

Line

40 King,] D; King all other copies

46 religion,] trace of Greg's comma in Hn, Bm
   Master's] Ed.; M. all copies; Master (Lancashire)

116 newes-thirsting] trace of hyphen in D

130 Concubine.] Ed.; Concubine, all copies

134 you.] Ed.; you all copies

243 penance:] penance all copies (at end of line, punctuation almost certainly left out for lack of room)

273 buble] Ed.; bubble (Hazlitt); pebble (Lancashire); puble all copies; seems to sort better with froth (earlier in the line) than pebble does

274 And] (Hazlitt); turned n all copies

275 thee] the B

276 [Aside] (Hazlitt)
    out!] (Hazlitt); out? all copies

277 JOHN:] Joh. D, Bm, Bv, F, Hd, Hn, S; Jh B

278 sonne,] Ed.; sonne all copies

308 help,] help Hn

317 KING:] Kin. period om. Hn

333 lands?] Ed.; lands all copies

359 Gloster to you] italicized all copies

376 WARDEN:] Ed.; Keep. all copies

379 WARDEN:] Ed.; Keep. all copies

407 win,] (Hazlitt); wiu, all copies

416 No,] comma faint in Bm, Bv, D, Hn, B

433 Waveney,] (Hazlitt); Aveney all copies; the y is on the margin in all copies, and the punctuation, most likely a comma, was obviously left out

437 adew,] Ed.; adew all copies

439 Faukenbridge?] Ed.; Faukenbridge all copies

455 Thames,] all copies

460 (s.d) SKINKE] Ed.; ital. all copies

498 Lord] L ital. all copies

501 Lord] L ital. all copies

505 night] Ed.; night. all copies

511 tyde] ty de B, Bm, Hn

523 Faukenbridge] Fau kenbridge all copies

529 tytty tytty] (Lancashire); tytty tytty, all copies

552 (s.d.) ROBERT] Robin all copies

560 antiquity] Ed.; antiqiuity all copies

573 BLOCKE:] Blo (per. om.) all copies

574 conjure] Conjure all copies

575 Will] will all copies

577 Blocks] Ed.; blocks all copies

580 expects] (Hazlitt) excepts all copies

585 Why] why all copies

598 He] he all copies
    minde,] Ed.; minde. all copies

620 Who] who all copies

623 BLOCKE:] Bls. all copies

662 hope.] Ed.; hope, all copies

703 Falcones] s faint Bm, Hd

707 How] how all copies

708 secretly.] (Hazlitt); secretly all copies

713 gone] (Hazlitt); grone all copies

715 As] as all copies

723 Hude] hude all copies

746 Solicite] (Hazlitt); Solicitie all copies

750 Why] why all copies

764 yee,] Ed.; ye (Lancashire); you all copies

785 another] a nother all copies

797 me] (Hazlitt); keepe farre all copies

822 'tis] Ed.; ti's all copies

839 againe?] Ed.; againe. all copies

899 And] and all copies

902 So. Porter] (Lancashire); So porter all copies

905 Moorton?] Ed.; Moorton. all copies

908 comfortlesse.] Ed.; comfortlesse, all copies

937 harsh] Bv, Hn, S, D; ha sh Bm, Hd, F, B

947 father] Ed.; father. all copies

957 out even now;] (Hazlitt); out, even now all copies

961 him!] (Lancashire); him and your tut-a-tut! (Hazlitt); him and you tut atut, all copies

977 inhort] (Lancashire); insort all copies

978 QUEENE:] Quce. Hn

981 I intreate] (Lancashire); intreate all copies

1000 QUEENE:] Quee all copies

1003 end,] Ed.; end all copies

1005 resolv'd.] Ed.; resoul'd. all copies

1008 nuptiall] Ed.; numptiall all copies

1015 child.] Ed.; child, all copies

1043 LANCASTER:] (Lancashire); Rich. all copies

1066 brought him hyther] Ed.; lacuna all copies

1080 ye] (Hazlitt); he all copies

1092 seditions] (Hazlitt); seditious all copies

1106 away.] Ed; away, all copies

1123 Pursevant] (Hazlitt); Pnrsevant all copies

1129 EXEUNTT.] all copies

1130 (s.d.) ROBERT] Robin all copies

1160 Onely] onely all copies

1170 on] Ed.; one all copies

1217 BLOCKE:] B. all copies

1258 shillings: heere] Ed.; shillings. heere all copies

1289 suspition] Ed.; suspitition all copies

1302 and't] (Lancashire); and be all copies

1308 GLOSTER:] (Hazlitt); Fau. all copies

1320 John, Prince] (Lancashire); John Prince, all copies
     JOHN:] Jo all copies

1374 Close] (Lancashire); Gloster, close all copies
     Gloster adieu] Gloste radieu all copies

1392 John:] Ed.; John all copies

1395 [for] Ed.; look it all copies

1412 shamelesse,] Ed.; shamelesse all copies

1413 Since,] Ed.; Since all copies

     Shiriffes,] Ed.; Siriffes, all copies

1447 RICHARD:] Rcih. all copies

1518 sicke;] Ed.; sicke, all copies

1523 DRAWER:] Dra, all copies

1541 Within] (Hazlitt); Withing all copies

1583 out of doors,] Ed.; out, of doors all copies

1606 lying] (Hazlitt); lyiug all copies

1608 pleasure] (Hazlitt); pleasnre all copies

1614 venterous] venterons S

1658 th'] Ed.; th'e all copies

1666 RICHARD:] Rcih. all copies
     sir?] Ed.; sir. all copies

1697 so] (Hazlitt); fo all copies

1735 fiends] (Lancashire); friends all copies

1745 art] (Hazlitt); at all copies

1749 (s.d.) ROBERT] Robin all copies

1770 indebted] Ed.; indepted all copies

1771-2 supper, Humphery. Pray looke about for Blocke,
Humphery.] (Lancashire); supper. Humphery, pray looke about
for Blocke, Humphery? all copies

1796 and s s see] (Hazlitt); ad s s see all copies

1816 hang'd] (Hazlitt); hang all copies

1824 as 'a] (Lancashire); as 't all copies

1820 friend.] Ed.; friend all copies

1878 honour'd] (Hazlitt); houour'd all copies

1928 wife.] Ed.; wife, all copies

1937 true?] Ed.; true, all copies
     If he himselfe] (Lancashire); Himself,/[If he] (Hazlitt);
Himselfe all copies

1944 chaine,] Ed.; chaine all copies

1957 Most] most all copies

1966 Stepney] stepney all copies

1970 be] (Hazlitt); by all copies

1983 him,] Ed.; larger than normal space after him all
copies

1985 He'll] he'll all copies

2009 not,] Ed.; not all copies

2046-8 Verse printed in quarto as prose

2053-4 Verse printed in quarto as prose

2056 take a theefe,] (Lancashire); take, all copies

2111 'twas] Ed.; wa's all copies

2130 invock'd] (Hazlitt); invocke all copies

2132 patients] Ed.; patience (Hazlitt); patient all copies

2139 me] Ed.; Assure he all copies

2140 FAUKENBRIDGE:] (Hazlitt); Gloster all copies

2146 Olde Knight winke] (Hazlitt); Olde winke all copies
     't may] Ed.; t'may all copies

2148 Prince John] (Hazlitt); Prince all copies

2152 JOHN:] F, D (written in); Glo. all other copies

2157 admire.] Ed.; admire, all copies

2176 RICHARD:] Bm; no prefix all other copies

2178 you] (Hazlitt); your all copies

2180 content.] Ed.; content, all copies

2182 ROBERT] Robin all copies

2200 for you] (Hazlitt); you for all copies

2204 joy] (Hazlitt); in all copies

2218 imposed] (Hazlitt); inposed all copies

2224 let not one] (Hazlitt); let one all copies

2256 woo'd] Ed.; wood all copies

2281 you.] Ed.; you, all copies

2287 made?] Ed.; made:? all copies

2309 In,] Ed.; In all copies

2317 prying] (Hazlitt); prining all copies

2320 women] (Hazlitt); wowen all copies

2345 us] (Hazlitt); as all copies

2348 ROBERT] Robin all copies

2351 Madam.] Ed.; Madam all copies

2352 ROBERT:] Hazlitt); La. all copies

2357 Call] Ed.; preceded by prefix La. all copies
     BLOCKE:] blocke all copies

2364 mynd.] Ed.; mynd, all copies

2365 ROBERT:] (Lancashire); La. all copies

2370 me. She] Ed.; me. she all copies

2390 John] Ed.; John, all copies

2429 Come] come all copies

2481 other's] (Hazlitt); other all copies

2516 wondrous] (Hazlitt); wondrours all copies

2523 ROBERT:] Robin all copies

2529 Huntington, be stil] (Hazlitt); Huntington, stil all
copies

2534 RICHARD:] (Hazlitt); Richard's speech begins at 2525 all
copies

2537 foyle] (Hazlitt); soyle all copies

2538 wreake] (Hazlitt); weake all copies

2544 thou] (Lancashire); then all copies

2579 Its] its all copies

2581 Stepney] stepney

2582 Adew] A dew all copies

2585 wary] (Hazlitt); wray all copies

2591 by] (Hazlitt); hy all copies

2615 t'one] (Hazlitt); tone all copies

2619 He] he all copies

2627 Hermit.] Ed.; Hermit, all copies

2629 budge.] Ed.; budge, all copies

2709 with myne] D (written in); missing all other copies

2722 tongue] Bm (written in by Steevens); tougue all other copies

2757 She's] (Hazlitt); He's all copies

2764 world] Ed.; word all copies

2768 Baffild] (Lancashire); Buffild all copies

2772 me] D (written in); om. all other copies

2777 we'l] wel all copies

2781 thither,] Ed.; thither all copies

2794 (s.d.) PRINCESSE] Princcsse all copies

2817 tw tw] Ed.; two to all copies

2836 coronation] Ed.; cornation all copies

2856 clear [eye] Ed.; Lancashire suggests beam, Hazlitt arch;
lacuna all copies

2885 doubt,] doubt Hn (probably faulty inking)

2908 he] (Hazlitt); om. all copies

2928 sir Richard] (Hazlitt); sir William all copies

2946 stammerer] (Lancashire); hammerer all copies

2961 resolv'd] (Lancashire); resoul'd all copies

2991 QUEENE:] Quee F

3000 woman:] woman, F
     their] there F

3002 spirit] Ed.; spirit, all copies

2993 Lift meek to thrones:] (Lancashire); Life, need, thrones:
all copies; Hazlitt suggests "Life kneels to thrones" in a
note, but prints the quarto line

3012 in a] in F

3015 execution] F; ex ecution all other copies

3022 mother] mothr F
     wil] will F

3029 knees,] knees F

3043 have drunke:] have: drunke F

3045 KING KNEELE DOWNE.] Kneele downe. F

3049 kneel'd] kneell'd F

3051 Take (as catchword on previous page)] take F

3070 [brings] Ed.; brought all copies

3095 as] (Hazlitt); is all copies

3097 Justice done.] (Hazlitt); Iustice all copies

3116 yee] Ed.; ye (Lancashire); you all copies

3126 off] (Lancashire); of all copies

3141 friends] friend F

3165 Wondrous] Wondrours F

3171 satisfaction] satisfaction, F

3183 valiant] valliant F

3195 crown'd] Ed.; crowned all copies

3196 Let's] (Lancashire); Lets' all copies

Set in Baskervill Old Face and
Imsai Elite. Designed
by G. R. Endel